D1419823

**Welfare Economics
in Theory and Practice**

Two week
loan

Please return on or before the last
date stamped below.
Charges are made for late return.

Macmillan books of related interest

P. J. Curwen and A. H. Fowler: ECONOMIC POLICY
Ajit K. Dasgupta and D. W. Pearce: COST–BENEFIT ANALYSIS
J. Harvey: MODERN ECONOMICS (2nd edn)
S. K. Nath: A PERSPECTIVE OF WELFARE ECONOMICS
D. W. Pearce: COST–BENEFIT ANALYSIS
Peter Self: ECONOCRATS AND THE POLICY PROCESS

Welfare Economics in Theory and Practice

CATHERINE M. PRICE

© Catherine M. Price 1977

First published 1977 by
THE MACMILLAN PRESS LTD
London and Basingstoke
Associated companies in New York Dublin
Melbourne Johannesburg and Madras

ISBN 0 333 19122 6 (hard cover)
     0 333 19838 7 (paper cover)

Text set in 11/12 pt Photon Imprint, printed by photolithography
and bound in Great Britain at The Pitman Press, Bath.

Contents

Preface

This book is intended for second- and third-year undergraduates and postgraduates who are studying the economic basis of public policy and is designed to provide a basic text for a variety of courses concerned with microeconomic decision-making. It assumes an elementary knowledge of the tools of economic analysis (at the level of an introductory course in the subject) but should prove useful to students who are not necessarily economic specialists. The author's main objective is to fill the gap which currently exists between highly specialised and involved works on economic theory and those with a more practical slant, by providing some progression from theory to practice. To achieve this, the book has been divided into three parts, each with four main chapters. Part One considers the theoretical implications of neoclassical welfare analysis, Part Two derives some policy guidelines, and Part Three uses four examples of practical issues to illustrate the ideas developed earlier. Of necessity the material presented is highly selective, and some readers will wish to examine particular aspects in greater depth; there are many more specialised works appropriate for such a purpose, some of which are listed in the bibliography. It is hoped that the present book will provide a useful background against which some of the more esoteric literature can be assessed in a broader context of theoretical and practical issues.

I am most grateful to my husband, Christopher, for preparing the diagrams and for his encouragement and tolerance which have enabled me to combine writing this book with my family commitments. I should also like to acknowledge help from Roger Nellist of the Department of Energy in commenting on Chapter 10, and from John Bates, senior lecturer in economics at Nottingham University, for discussing Part Two, and for inspiring and guiding my original interest in welfare economics.

I hope that this book may help its readers to discover for themselves some of the fascination which I have found in the area of theoretical analysis and public policy.

Part One

Theory

Chapter 1

The Basis of Welfare Economics

The welfare of an individual or community can be defined as its well-being, or, more picturesquely, its attainment of bliss. Welfare economics is concerned with the effect of economic policies on the level of welfare of individuals or groups of people. The analysis is used to compare the relative merits of two situations by assessing the level of welfare in each, and in doing so is dependent on a variety of conventional economic tools. However, this branch of the subject differs from the purely descriptive analysis of other economic approaches by attempting to ascertain how far one position is *better* than another rather than in merely identifying the characteristics of each. In this sense welfare economics is normative in prescribing recommendations and not purely positive (or descriptive) like much of the subject matter in economics. Thus, while an empirical approach might show the Government the likely effects of different investment programmes, a welfare economist would attempt to combine these forecasts with a set of priorities to recommend a particular project as yielding greater welfare than the alternatives.

In analysing proposals in this way the welfare economist clearly has to work closely with Government and others who are responsible for determining in what direction society's interests lie. An economist's own political views on how welfare or the effects of changes should be distributed amongst the community are no more significant than any other citizen's so that his analysis should be generally acceptable in the context in which it is used (though the conclusion drawn from it by any individual may be idiosyncratic). Unfortunately such agreement is not always easy to achieve; for example, in the Commission on London's third airport, discussed in Chapter 12, the relative valuation of monetary benefits of inland sites and the smaller incursion into local residents' life by Foulness could not be agreed within the Commission, so that Professor Buchanan published a minority report disagreeing with his colleagues' conclusions. Similarly the exploitation of North Sea oil, which forms the subject of Chapter 10, has controversial aspects, especially to the Scottish Nationalist Party, which feels the resources should be used for Scotland's benefit rather than to increase the welfare of the United Kingdom as a whole. In these discussions it is the task of the economist to build up some analysis to compare the welfare of different alternatives on the basis of priorities suggested by Government or arrived at by consensus. Of course the basic premise on which he bases his conclusions affects the validity of his recommendations. Indeed the desire to produce analysis acceptable to as many parties as possible while still arriving at meaningful conclusions forms one of the main dilemmas of welfare economics.

Welfare has been defined as a measure of well-being, and it is difficult to be more precise about its nature. Utility is sometimes used as a synonym, though this has the disadvantage of implying (misleadingly) that it arises only from the consumption of 'useful' goods rather than from more frivolous pursuits which give pleasure. Contributing to welfare are a galaxy of conditions which may be defined as constituting the 'quality of life', for example security, protection from fear, electoral freedom, a 'sense of purpose', as well as the more obvious economic factors like income and price levels. An economic policy which changes any factor contributing to welfare is the concern of welfare economics in deciding whether the community is better or worse off as a result. In doing so the obvious starting point is how an individual is affected by change.

An individual's well-being is obviously a personal and idiosyncratic function of the factors which make up his environment (though each consumer's choices must be internally consistent within his own framework of preferences if they are to be subject to meaningful analysis). For example, one man may be deeply distressed by being made redundant while another may find it beneficial to receive redundancy pay and the opportunity to seek another job (the fact that many firms offer employees the chance to volunteer for redundancy before they enforce lay-offs shows that they recognise the different effects on different members of the work-force). Again, one family may be oblivious of the material possessions of their neighbours while others are anxiously 'keeping up with the Jones's', and feel less well off if the Jones's acquire a better car or colour television. It thus appears virtually impossible for anyone else to determine just how an economic change in his own or others' circumstances is likely to affect the utility of an individual; the only sure guide is his own assessment of whether welfare increases or declines. Most people do know whether or not they feel themselves to be better off when circumstances change, and may reveal this in observable behaviour, for example by seeking to move house if they are adversely affected by the noise from an airport. However, very few could adequately quantify a welfare change even though they know its direction, for it is a subjective magnitude which is not readily measurable in other terms. The worker who welcomes redundancy, for example, might say he felt his welfare was raised by the chance to seek alternative employment, and might experience a further increase in welfare on finding a suitable vacancy. But it is unlikely that he could compare the increases in welfare (except so far as they involve money changes) and it would not be feasible to compare his gain in welfare with the distress of his colleague who resisted redundancy. Thus an absolute measure of welfare is unlikely to be appropriate even for comparing changes in a single individual's utility, let alone for welfare comparisons *between* citizens. However, it would be misleading to suggest that because of these difficulties interpersonal utility comparisons are never made, for sometimes it may seem to be the only way of achieving positive policy conclusions. In particular cost–benefit analysis, whose principles are discussed in Chapter 8, depends on the ability to assess the amount of compensation which members of the community require to return them to the same level of welfare as before a particular change. This does not strictly constitute a measure of welfare as such, since the compensation depends on other economic variables (income level, relative prices, and so on) but is an attempt to provide a monetary measure of welfare changes. It is based on the theory of compensation, outlined in Chapter 2, and this in turn requires only the existence of an ordinal utility measure, that is one in which an individual can *rank* states according to his well-being, but cannot say by *how much* his welfare varies in different situations.

The inability to measure individual utility in absolute terms leads to difficulty in assessing the welfare effects of any change on the whole community from knowledge of how it influences the constituent members. For while an individual cannot express his welfare in absolute terms it is impossible to aggregate changes in community welfare without making judgements about the relative merits of distribution patterns. If utility were measurable in cardinal terms and different individuals' welfare could be compared, then it would be possible to add the total utility experienced by each member to know the community welfare in different cases. However, such interpersonal comparisons are not possible if there is no absolute measure of welfare. To proceed from individual effects to community implications some distributional judgements are necessary so that community welfare can be derived from that of the individuals who comprise it. For example, if one policy is likely to bring advantages to stockbrokers, and an alternative to benefit coalminers, how are comparisons to be made? Clearly, if it is possible to increase the welfare of every individual, this would raise community welfare, but it is difficult to draw clear conclusions in other cases.

One approach to this problem is to construct a social-welfare function (see, for example, Bergson [1966]), which relates the over-all welfare of the community to all the factors which might affect it. It is evident from the argument above that this can only be achieved by incorporating distributional judgements (for example about the relative merits of increases in stockbrokers' and coalminers' welfare) and these may present considerable difficulties. For under democratic Government (and probably also in totalitarian regimes) it is virtually impossible to gain consensus about the distribution of income, let alone to obtain the information in such a way that it can be quantified and incorporated in a model to relate community to individual welfare. To be operative such a model should be capable of giving some figure for welfare levels in different situations so that the positions can be compared to see which yields greater benefits. In practice such a social-welfare function is virtually impossible either to construct or to operate.

However, what may be feasible is to identify and analyse a particular aspect of the social-welfare function, for example the characteristic mentioned earlier that community welfare would rise if that of every member were to increase. This is the basic premise of the work of an Italian political economist, Vilfredo Pareto. He wrote at the turn of the century, and although this was before the general revival of interest in welfare economics in the 1930s, it became the basis of what was developed then as the neoclassical approach. It is perhaps unfortunate in the interests of dispassionate assessment of his economic analysis that Pareto took a conservative elitist view of political theory and was associated with right-wing politics. His economic theory has been accused of similar bias and has sometimes been used to support policies traditionally associated with conservative Government. It will become evident from the implications of his analysis that the results could be used in this way, though this is more likely to be because of bias in the interpretation than in the theory itself. This has been used to form the basis of much of modern welfare economic analysis, and should be considered according to its own merits and limitations.

Pareto's work (see the recent edition [1972]) is based on the contention that distributional judgements are best avoided altogether since it is difficult to obtain consensus about them, they do not lend themselves easily to incorporation in an analytical framework, and particular assumptions would limit the applicability of conclusions based upon them. Instead he defined an improvement in community welfare only if it involved an increase in the utility of at least one individual and a decrease in the utility of none. Such a change is seen as an increase in efficiency, and Pareto defined a position of maximum efficiency as one in which no one could be made better off without someone becoming worse off. (Note that this is not necessarily a position of maximum *welfare* as later discussion and Figure 4 show, though efficiency in this sense is sometimes referred to as *Paretian welfare*.) His approach was a comparative-static analysis with a given quantity of resources, but, as the discussion in Chapter 4 shows, there are no problems in principle which prevent the extension to a dynamic economy. Pareto's analysis maintains near-universal acceptability by avoiding any controversial distributional judgement, though only by ignoring altogether this important facet of welfare. The danger is to grasp too firmly what seems a concrete and reasonable aspect of economic welfare from the morass of conditions which affect society's well-being, and to over-emphasise its theoretical and practical importance because it lends itself to analytical development. The other factors which contribute to welfare are no less important because they are not conveniently analysed, and in examining the efficiency of any particular situation such considerations must be taken into account; often this can only be done intuitively, and not analytically, though one serious attempt to include the effects of changes in the quality of life has been made in cost–benefit analysis, based on comparisons of consumers' surplus, which is discussed later in the book. If such considerations are always ignored, the critics of Paretian economics seem justified in their accusations of narrow-mindedness, though this is a criticism of the application rather than of the analysis. It is important to remember the limits of any approach in assessing its usefulness as a tool for comparing the relative merits of two situations.

The development of Pareto's principles into conditions which define a position of maximum efficiency is familiar to most students of economics, and is based on the proposition that in such an optimum situation it is impossible to redistribute resources so that one individual (or production process) can obtain greater satisfaction (output) except at the expense of another unit of the economy. Thus a number of marginal conditions must exist if a redistribution to make someone better off without anyone becoming worse off is impossible, and these have been neatly summarised by K. E. Boulding [1948] as follows:

(i) if transformation from one economic variable to another is possible then the rate of indifferent substitution between them must be equal to the rate of technical substitution; and

(ii) all equivalent rates of technical and indifferent substitution must be equal.

It may highlight the implications of the summary above to consider a simple example in which they are not satisfied and efficiency could be improved. One of the policies discussed later in the book (in general terms in Chapter 7 and more specifically in Chapter 11) is marginal-cost pricing. If the price of a train journey, say, is set above the marginal cost of transporting a passenger for that journey (ignoring any problems of cost estimation), some consumers who would have travelled at a price equal to the marginal cost will not be prepared to pay the higher price and so will not travel by train. Some of these consumers would have been prepared to pay a maximum price higher than marginal cost but less than the set price. These travellers would benefit if prices were fixed at marginal cost, and the railway operators would not suffer since their extra (marginal) costs are recovered from revenues received. Thus it would be more efficient on these grounds to institute marginal-cost pricing, which would satisfy Pareto's criterion in this transaction. For a situation in which all prices are equal to marginal costs and each consumer allocates income to maximise his utility the ratio of marginal utilities between each pair of products is the same for all consumers and equals the ratio of their marginal costs. Thus one set of Paretian conditions is satisfied.

In some circumstances the criteria may need some re-interpretation. One arises in the case of joint products, when there are necessarily two outputs from a single production process. If the proportion in which they are produced is variable, then a marginal rate of technical substitution between them can be defined, but where it is fixed no such entity exists since both must be produced together in given proportions. In either case the marginal conditions for technical and indifferent substitution must be altered, for it is necessary that the total satisfaction rendered by the production process should be compared with the necessary inputs, and not just the satisfaction from one of the products. An example arises in the search for North Sea oil, or indeed in mining any minerals, where the result of exploitation is often a number of different products, in this case oils of different fractions and suitable for different uses. Here there is likely to be some variability in the proportion of various distillates produced, but this is limited by the type of crude oil discovered. Then it is the sum of the various rates of substitution between each output and any other good that should be brought into equality to satisfy the spirit of Paretian efficiency conditions. For optimum efficiency the sum of the marginal rate of substitution between each of the joint products and any other should equal the marginal rate of transformation between that product and the joint output. The same principle should be applied to joint products in consumption. Such a case arises in aircraft and aviation fuel, where both are used together to yield utility to consumers travelling by air. If maximum efficiency is to be reached it is necessary that the relative merits of the marginal use of both together and any other good should equal the joint marginal use of resources. Thus the sum of the marginal rates of transformation between the aircraft and the fuel and any other product must be equal to the rate of indifferent substitution between plane and fuel *together* and that product. In each case of joint products (in production or consumption) Pareto's conditions should be extended to incorporate the sum of the relevant marginal rates in calculating ratios.

A similar case in which marginal conditions need modification arises for 'public goods', that is those whose consumption by one individual does not affect their use by another. The classic example of such a product is radio and television transmission, which can be received by anyone with suitable equipment regardless of who else is also listening or watching. Similarly there are public 'bads', for example a transistor radio tuned in at loud volume in a public place to a programme others within earshot may not wish to hear. In both these cases it is the total effect of each 'act of production' which is important in determining the ratio of relevant rates of substitution, that is the sum of the effects on each individual who enjoys or detests the consequences of radio transmission. Thus, in comparing the marginal rate of indifferent substitution between reception of radio broadcasts and other goods, with corresponding marginal rates of technical substitution, the sum over all consumers affected should be estimated. Otherwise, in considering the advantage of transmission to only a single consumer, there would be opportunity to increase efficiency by asking other beneficiaries to finance further broadcasts, while ignoring the adverse effects of noise pollution might suggest that more loud programmes would be broadcast in public than would result in maximum efficiency.

The adjustments to Pareto's criteria suggested above are straightforward in principle but may be much less so in practice. It is often difficult to be sure how far effects do persist through the economy. In particular it is difficult to allow for them in the absence of markets which can be relied upon to bring private consequences of any action into equality with its social results. Many students will be familiar with the Paretian marginal conditions because they are satisfied in general equilibrium of a perfectly competitive economy in which private and social costs coincide. However, such analysis does involve further assumptions than have yet been incorporated about the nature of economic decisions, since the marginal conditions are only brought into the requisite ratios if each consumer seeks to maximise his utility and producers maximise profits, that is each unit acts rationally (though not necessarily consciously) in promoting his own welfare. There has been some doubt as to how far such an assumption is sensible. J. K. Galbraith [1974] in particular has criticised its validity in modern economics where consumers' preferences may be rendered unstable by advertising pressure. However, it is difficult to know what other assumptions about consumer behaviour are reasonable, and if any market mechanism which relies on freedom of economic choice operates, the only sensible basis of analysis seems to be that each individual maximises his welfare within the limits imposed on him by the system. This assumption will be incorporated in analysis of production and consumption choices in this book, despite the above criticisms of such an approach and the writer's own lack of conviction that this is how *all* decisions are reached. If a more comprehensive analytical base were available, this might be preferable, but in its absence utility and profit maximisation seem reasonable and acceptable assumptions.

The coincidence of Pareto's criteria with those achieved in perfect competition, often the first market form the student of economics analyses, should not lead him to suppose that it is therefore the only one which can yield maximum efficiency. In theory, at least, it would be possible in a command economy to direct resources so that the conditions were met. The practical problems involved in doing so would be immense, but a perfectly competitive economy is also unlikely in practice. In examining Pareto's approach it is important, too, to remember its limits, since even if maximum efficiency *could* be achieved in a market or command economy, it might not be desirable if other considerations, such as equity, indicated that higher welfare might be gained by sacrificing efficiency to alternative ends. It will become clear in later chapters that, in practice, it is most unusual for Pareto's criteria to be fully satisfied and that this has implications for both efficiency and other aspects of welfare. However, for the time being, we consider some more technical disadvantages of the marginal conditions which define maximum efficiency.

One problem is that the marginal conditions necessary for maximum efficiency also define a minimum; this is unlikely to cause difficulty in practice since once a turning point is identified from the marginal conditions, inspection of the possibility of redistributing resources locally should indicate whether it is a position of maximum or minimum Paretian welfare. A simple example of how the marginal conditions identify both maximum and minimum efficiency points arises in classical production theory, when a firm determines the optimum combination of inputs to yield a given output. With a given price ratio between two factors of production the most efficient combination of factors is at the point where the rate of exchange between them in the market (the slope of the isocost curve) equals the rate of transformation between them in production (slope of the isoquant), that is at M in Figure 1. However, the isoquant continues beyond the ridge lines (where the marginal return to each factor becomes negative) and curves back on itself, showing that with a sufficient quantity of factors yielding negative returns the same total output is achieved, though of course at much greater cost. Indeed the point of maximum cost (minimum efficiency) is at N, where an isocost is again tangential to the production function, though this time at maximum rather than minimum distance from the origin. So N also satisfies the marginal conditions for most efficient production, although it represents minimum efficiency. This shows clearly how unimportant such a theoretical coincidence may be in practice, for it is inconceivable that a producer would continue to add factors of production when they yield negative returns, that is beyond the ridge lines. It is only if the marginal conditions are applied dogmatically and without thought for their interpretation that this problem might become significant.

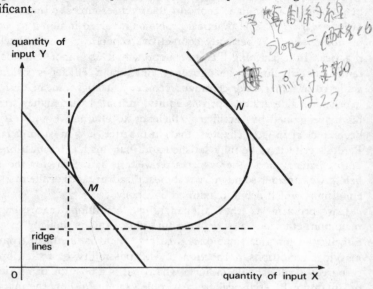

FIGURE 1

Two other difficulties which can occur in applying the marginal conditions may be more serious, and both arise from the local nature of any examination at the margin. The first is that there may be a number of positions of *local* welfare maximisation, that is situations in which small redistributions of resources can only yield increased satisfaction to some at the expense of others. The marginal conditions will be satisfied at all such positions of local maximum welfare, and Pareto's criterion by itself gives no guide as to which maximum welfare position should be the objective, particularly where each involves a different distribution of income. This comparison must be made by some competent authority within the economy, usually the Government, and may involve non-efficiency considerations; the danger lies in achieving a local position of maximum efficiency and concentrating on its maintenance when a situation of higher welfare could have been achieved by moving away from this local op-

timum and aiming for the *optimum optimorum*, that is the Paretian
efficient point which yields greatest over-all welfare. Economic
analysis is traditionally presented in such a way that these difficulties
are not illustrated; for example, the production function and the
isocost curve are depicted as having a single well-defined point of
maximum efficiency at which production should take place, and for the
consumer unique relative prices prevail which give a single position of
tangency between a budget line and a smooth indifference curve.
However, in practice these assumptions of classical analysis may not
be achieved and the marginal conditions then become an ambiguous
guide to maximum efficiency. Consider the not uncommon situation in
which a consumer choosing between two goods is faced with a discount on one product if he buys more than a certain quantity. This
arises in energy purchases and might be relevant in the choice between
gas and electricity; domestic tariffs usually depend on the amount of
fuel bought, with a cheaper price available to consumers who buy
larger amounts. Thus the consumer faces different relative prices according to the quantity purchased. A very simple example could be illustrated as in Figure 2 by supposing that a discount is available if
more than $0X$ units of electricity are bought, so that the budget line
takes the shape $ABCD$, illustrating the relatively cheaper price of electricity beyond B. (When X is first reached the budget line becomes
horizontal indicating that at the cheaper price more units of electricity

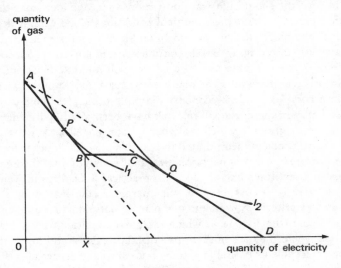

FIGURE 2

can be bought without spending more money than was needed to buy $0X$ units at the higher price.) If the consumer wishes to maximise his satisfaction, that is reach the highest indifference curve for a particular budget line, Pareto's principles show that he will do so at the point where the rate of exchange in the market (slope of the budget line) is equal to his indifferent rate of substitution between the goods (slope of the indifference curve). Thus maximum efficiency in allocating his income is achieved at the point of tangency between the curves. However, in the case of a dual-price budget line there may be two such positions, namely P and Q as illustrated in Figure 2.

Clearly Q represents higher welfare for this individual since it lies on I_2, an indifference curve further from the origin than I_1 on which P lies. If the consumer recognises both Q and P as possible optimum positions he will also realise that Q yields him greater utility, and he will allocate his income accordingly. However, if he finds himself at P and applies only local criteria, considering how *small* changes in purchases of the two goods along the budget line would affect his welfare, he will conclude that changes will yield him lower satisfaction by placing him on lower indifference curves, and so perhaps miss altogether the existence of point Q.

The case discussed above is a very simple and not unusual example, and applies only to an individual maximising welfare rather than to the problem of allocating resources between individuals within a society. However, it should illustrate how more than one local maximum position can arise, and that marginal conditions alone cannot define which is the most efficient. No such 'oddities' as indifference curves concave to the origin, or discontinuous or kinked production-possibility curves, are needed to produce such multiple local optima, and in practice there must be many positions of maximum efficiency within a complex modern economy. Pareto's principles alone cannot choose between them, though once all have been identified it may be clear on other grounds which will yield greater benefits to society.

The third problem incorporated in Paretian analysis arises from the limited nature of the original principles, and though of little theoretical interest it constitutes one of the main practical difficulties in welfare comparisons. It occurs because the marginal efficiency conditions provide only criteria by which to compare an optimum position with a non-optimum (that is one in which marginal conditions are satisfied with one where they are not). In practice, however, an optimum may not be achievable or desirable if some non-efficiency aspect of welfare (for example equity in income distribution or an imperfection in the markets) prevents the attainment of an optimum; indeed it is likely that this will often be the case, and Pareto's conditions give no criterion by which to compare sub-optimal situations. For example, two individuals A and B, who are trading in an Edgeworth box situation of fixed amounts of two goods, X and Y, will achieve maximum efficiency on the 'contract curve' (the locus of points of tangency of their two sets of indifference curves where these are mapped from diagonally opposite corners of the box as origins; see Figure 3).

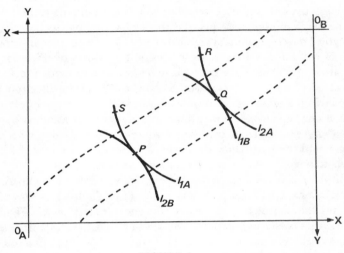

FIGURE 3

Pareto's marginal conditions show that any point on the contract curve is more efficient than any point not on it, since the curve represents the locus of points at which the rate of indifferent substitution between goods X and Y is the same for both members of society. At any point not on the contract curve, say S, it is possible to redistribute resources to increase efficiency. For example, by moving to P, A would be no worse off since this is on the same indifference curve (I_{1A}) as S, but P is on an indifference curve further from B's origin and so he will have greater utility at P than at S. Thus the move from S to P would constitute an improvement according to Paretian criteria. But these conditions cannot indicate which is the most efficient attainable position if for some reason (perhaps the imposition of indirect taxes or some other interference in the market system) the area between the dotted lines, including the free-bargain contract curve, is unattainable. Which of the still realisable sub-optimal positions is best is not encompassed by the efficiency criteria; for example, there is no way of using the Paretian analysis to compare the relative merits of S and R in Figure 3. Yet it is most often only such sub-optimal positions which can be reached in a mixed economy, and about just such points which welfare judgements need to be made. This difficulty is discussed further in a theoretical context in Chapter 3 which deals with the 'second best'.

This chapter has attempted to introduce the student to the ideas and objectives of welfare economics and to examine the technicalities of the Paretian approach. Because this lends itself particularly well to analytical development and application it is inevitable that any discussion of economic welfare concentrates on this aspect of efficiency and the attempts which have been made to extend its practical use. One pitfall of viewing this approach too narrowly can be illustrated by comparing Pareto-optimal situations with wider welfare considerations. For example, the analysis illustrated in Figures 2 and 3 above gives no way of comparing sub-optimal positions with each other; neither can it define the *optimum optimorum*, or 'best' Paretian efficient point – which can only be determined by introducing distribution judgements. It is impossible, for example, to compare the welfare associated with positions P and Q in Figure 3, or anywhere else on the contract curve, from efficiency criteria alone. Figure 4 shows that welfare priorities may be such that, in practice, some points yield greater over-all welfare than others which are more efficient. For simplicity a two-person community is shown with the utility experienced by each member measured along the axes. The points of maximum efficiency can be represented by a continuous curve (equivalent to the contract curve) which will normally be concave to the origin. Every point on this curve PP represents a Paretian optimum. On the same diagram can be represented contours of the over-all welfare function which we have supposed to exist (although its precise nature is difficult to determine) convex to the origin, those further from the origin representing greater community welfare. Three such contours, W_1, W_2, W_3, are shown in Figure 4.

Q, the point of tangency between PP and a welfare contour, clearly represents the *optimum optimorum*; but T and U are also Pareto-efficient, and it is interesting to note that S, although not a point of maximum efficiency since it does not lie on PP, represents higher welfare than T (which is Pareto-efficient) since it is on a higher welfare contour. Of course if it were possible to define welfare contours in practice as in this hypothetical example, society could merely aim for the point Q and establish maximum welfare. As this is impracticable the welfare economist must grope towards such a position as best he can with the tools available to him. What this example seeks to emphasise is the danger of becoming too immersed in efficiency

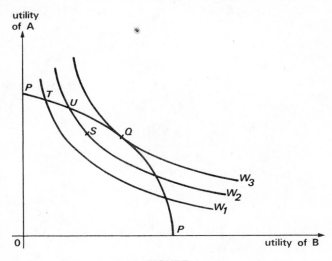

FIGURE 4

criteria and aiming for a particular Pareto optimum, say T, at the expense of wider aspects of economic welfare, better served at S, which is not Pareto optimal. It is this very restrictiveness of Pareto's approach which contributes both to its usefulness as a precise analytical tool and to the pitfalls of narrow-mindedness in its application. Many attempts to extend its applicability without losing its universality have been made, though not often with success since the temptation to incorporate implicit assumptions in such extensions is difficult to resist. Some particularly strongly debated ideas on extending the scope of the analysis are outlined in the next chapter.

Suggestions for Further Reading

ABRAM BERGSON, *Essays in Normative Economics* (The Belknap Press of Harvard University Press, 1966).

K. E. BOULDING, 'Welfare Economics', in *A Survey of Contemporary Economics*, vol. 2, ed. American Economic Association (Blakiston, 1948).

J. K. GALBRAITH, *The New Industrial State,* 2nd edn (Harmondsworth: Penguin, 1974).

I. M. D. LITTLE, *A Critique of Welfare Economics* (Oxford University Press, 1957).

NANCY RUGGLES, 'Recent Developments in the Theory of Marginal Cost Pricing', *Review of Economic Studies,* vol. 17 (1949–50).

D. M. WINCH, *Analytical Welfare Economics* (Harmondsworth: Penguin, 1971).

Chapter 2

The Compensation Principle

Extension of Pareto's conditions was attempted when N. Kaldor [1939] discussed a change which improved the welfare of some members of the community only at the cost of others. Here was a situation in which Pareto's principles could not help directly, since if any suffer from a change, welfare comparisons can be made only by involving distributional judgements which Pareto particularly avoided. Unfortunately in practice most economic decisions involve just such combinations of loss and gain; changes which incur only benefits for all members of society are usually undertaken without needing specific economic analysis. Problems arise when gain for one sector of society can be achieved only at the cost of decreased welfare for another.

Discussion about compensation centred initially on the decision to repeal the Corn Laws in the nineteenth century; this repeal did not improve welfare in the Paretian sense since although large numbers benefited by having cheaper bread some farmers were worse off because the price of corn had been lowered. Kaldor maintained that if those who benefited from the repeal were so much better off that they could have afforded to compensate the farmers for their loss, and yet still be in a better position than before the change in the law, then the repeal of the Corn Laws represented an increase in welfare for the country as a whole, even if the compensation was not actually handed over.

If full compensation is paid then no controversy arises, since the 'losers' are compensated and so the conditions for a Paretian improvement are directly satisfied, with some gaining and none losing. However, for a situation in which the gainers *could* compensate the losers, but do not do so, welfare judgements involve assumptions far beyond those which Pareto himself was prepared to undertake. These arise in two ways. First, the compensation which a loser requires or a gainer is prepared to sacrifice so that he feels himself just as well off as before the change depends on his total level of well-being, that is on the distribution of income. (Since we assume that the marginal utility of money decreases, an individual measures his loss of utility as greater in money terms if he has a higher level of income.) Thus in accepting these personal assessments of changes in utility in money terms (and it is difficult to know how else to measure them) the economist accepts that the distribution of income is satisfactory. Consider, for example, a new road which affects two houses by a compulsory-purchase order on part of their gardens. Suppose that the inconvenience is judged to be similar by each family, that they are similarly placed in terms of family circumstances and that it affects equally the value of their properties. The poorer family may be prepared to settle for a lower compensation, even though their loss of utility seems equal to that of their rich neighbours, because the utility of the money they receive is greater and their lives might be made easier by increased expenditure on food, clothes or household equipment. Their richer neighbours may already have such items and therefore require more money to buy goods giving them equal utility to that lost by the road scheme. (Some of the practical problems of assessing the effect of development schemes on residential housing are discussed in Chapter 12 on the siting of the third London airport.) Clearly using monetary compensation as a measure of utility loss or gain implies acceptance of the current distribution of income.

Since in practice the welfare economist has to make some assumptions about the economic system (as we shall see in later chapters), supposing that the distribution of income is reasonable, or at least that the Government is fairly satisfied with the status quo, may not seem outrageous. More important is the second implicit assumption in Kaldor's compensation principle, that the redistribution of income from losers to gainers which results from the change is also satisfactory. Kaldor suggested that when the Corn Laws were repealed only the total change in utility was relevant even though it involved a redistribution of welfare from growers of corn to consumers of bread.

A stronger assumption is needed to judge that a particular change in distribution is desirable than to accept that the prevailing share of utility is satisfactory. In the example used it might be generally agreed that a redistribution from the comparatively rich farmers to the poorer consumers on a staple diet of bread was desirable, thus enhancing a change already thought beneficial.

However, a proposed project might equally well benefit a particularly wealthy section of the community at the expense of a poorer group. Here two assumptions incorporated in the analysis would tend to reinforce each other: the measure of gain to the rich in monetary terms tends to be inflated by the low marginal utility of their income, while compensation required by losers would be disproportionately low because of their higher marginal utility of money; and if the compensation were not paid a redistribution of welfare in favour of the rich would have occurred, contrary to the prevalent view in society that any redistribution should occur in the opposite direction. Therefore use of Kaldor's compensation principle in which compensation is not paid should be clearly distinguished from Paretian principles; for while it is claimed to be an extension of them, it introduces far stronger assumptions than Pareto was prepared to make. These can be justified to some extent by knowledge that the Government has other means at its disposal (income taxes for example) to alter any undesirable redistribution of income and that the welfare judgements involved are merely to assess the efficiency of a change. In any case some assumptions are necessary to extend the analytical tools to a wider and more useful sphere; but there should be no illusions that these are merely additions to the original ideas which do not change their nature.

The compensation principle has been presented as Kaldor originally proposed it, but it was somewhat altered after further comment. J. R. Hicks [1939] pointed out that a contradiction might arise from Kaldor's criterion; this could show that a change would constitute an improvement in welfare since those who were better off after the change would have more than enough 'extra welfare' to compensate the losers; and yet after the change a consideration of whether to reverse it would suggest that the original position represented higher welfare since those better off before the change had sufficient extra utility to compensate individuals whose welfare was higher after it. This anomaly arises because the compensation calculated under each change is not paid, and so if the redistribution of welfare between situations A and B is sufficient both the 'pro-A' and the 'pro-B' parties may have adequate surplus to compensate the losers in each case.

(Students who are familiar with the 'index-number problem' may recognise this as a familiar phenomenon, since the anomaly is analogous to that in which $\Sigma p_0 q_1 > \Sigma p_0 q_0$ and yet $\Sigma p_1 q_1 \leqslant \Sigma p_1 q_0$; see, for example, Braybrooke [1954–5].) The possible contradiction which Hicks pointed out would lead to some situations in which it appears both that A represented higher welfare than B and that B was a better position than A, which would not be helpful in decision-making. Hicks therefore suggested that a more negative criterion be substituted for Kaldor's condition to judge whether a change is an improvement, namely that the losers should not be able to compensate the gainers and still be better off than they would have been after the change. It was not until later that Tibor Scitovsky [1941–2] pointed out that in fact both the Hicks and the Kaldor conditions need to be satisfied if a change is to be unambiguously declared an improvement, and a simple example provided by Quirk and Saposnik [1968] neatly illustrates this possibility. They consider a two-person two-good economy in which each individual, (1) and (2), prefers to have one unit of each good, x and y, to two of one and none of the other, and receives positive marginal utility from each product. Now suppose that the two states to be considered, A and B, represent the following distributions of resources (where q_x and q_y are the quantities of x and y possessed by each individual).

	State A		State B	
Individual	q_x	q_y	q_x	q_y
(1)	1	0	2	0
(2)	0	2	0	1

Consider first Kaldor's rule for comparing the two states. (1) is better off in state B than in state A for he has more of q_x, and by giving (2) one unit of x he could remain just as well off as in state A while making (2) better off in state B (since the latter prefers one unit each of x and y to two units of y). Thus using Kaldor's criterion B represents higher welfare than A. However, if we now consider Hicks's approach we discover that individual (2), by giving one unit of y to (1) in state A could make (1) better off in state A than in state B and remain himself with the same welfare in each state. So, according to Hicks's rule, A is better than B.

Another way of illustrating these contradictions is diagrammatically (see Figures 5–8) where U_A and U_B represent possible combinations in states A and B of the utilities of the two members of the community. Each change involves a move from P to Q, where Q represents higher welfare for (2) and lower welfare for (1). Figures 5 and 8 show cases in which the revised compensation principle yields an unambiguous answer. For in Figure 5, (1) could be compensated by moving to position S, a redistribution in situation B which leaves both individuals better off and satisfies Paretian criteria for an improvement, while it is not possible to find any point on U_A which yields greater welfare to both parties than does Q. Thus the loser could not bribe the gainer from the change to forgo his improvement. Conversely, Figure 8 shows a change in which it is impossible for (2) to offer (1) as much as he receives at A without making himself worse off, while (1) can persuade (2) to forgo his advantages from the change by redistributing resources along U_A to R. Thus the move to Q would clearly cause a decline in community welfare. However, the intermediate figures (6 and 7) show more ambiguous situations. For in Figure 6, while (2) could persuade (1) to accept the change without detriment to himself by redistributing in state B to S, (1) might similarly prevail upon (2) to forgo the change by redistributing in state A to R. Thus Kaldor's conditions for an improvement are satisfied but Hicks's are not. Conversely, Figure 7 shows a case where Hicks's conditions are met but Kaldor's are not. For the loser (1) cannot find a position on U_A which will offer each as much utility as Q, and so persuade (2) to forgo the change; but neither can (2) find a position in B in which he can compensate (1) for his loss of utility and still himself have a net gain from the change. In cases where such ambiguity arises the conclusion as to which state represents higher community welfare is indeterminate unless additional explicit assumptions about distribution of welfare between individuals are incorporated. It is only if both Kaldor's and Hicks's conditions are satisfied that the change can unambiguously be judged an improvement, and the final form of the compensation principle, known as the Kaldor–Hicks–Scitovsky criterion, can be formulated as follows. A change from one situation to another may be judged an improvement if, and only if, both the following conditions are satisfied:

(*a*) the gainers from the change could have compensated the losers for their loss and still remain better off themselves; and

(*b*) the losers from the change could not have compensated the gainers for their forgone increase in welfare without themselves being worse off than in the original situation.

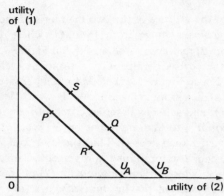

FIGURE 5

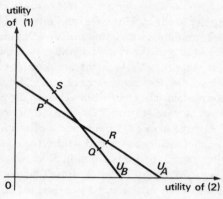

FIGURE 6

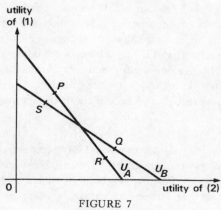

FIGURE 7

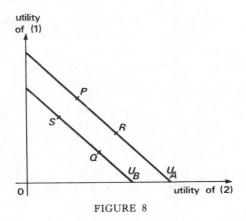

FIGURE 8

Although a little more refined than Kaldor's original suggestion, this principle still incorporates the bold assumptions about distribution and redistribution of income that have already been noted, and constitutes a significant new development of Paretian principles.

The assessment of the amount of compensation by which an individual measures a change in his welfare can be approached in various ways. The most theoretically satisfactory is probably via the ordinal utility assumptions incorporated in indifference curves, which can then be used to develop more practical measures. Perhaps the easiest way to illustrate the concepts involved is by considering the effect on the utility level of a consumer of a particular product whose price falls. This decline in price then has two effects on the individual concerned: it decreases the price of the good relative to others the consumer might buy, and it also increases his real income by raising the total quantity of goods he can command with a given money income. These effects are respectively the substitution and income effects, and can be illustrated by consideration of an individual's set of indifference curves between the good, X, and income Y (see Figure 9). Suppose the consumer initially faces a price P_2 which enables him to buy quantity X_1 of X if he spends all his income (M_2), but that the price then falls to P_1, so that he can buy X_2 units of X. Then the budget lines he faces in each case are M_2X_1 and M_2X_2 respectively. He maximises utility by choosing first A on U_1 and later, at a higher level, B on U_2. Then the move from A to B can be divided into two steps by finding point D on the original utility curve, the point at which a line with the same slope as MX_2 is tangent to U_1. This point is a position of equilibrium representing the same relative prices as after the change but the same utility level as before. Thus the move from A to D is a substitution effect, taking account only of changes in relative prices, while DB represents a change in utility at constant relative prices. In money terms the distance DB can be measured by the distance between the relevant income lines on the vertical axis, that is M_1M_2. This is known as the compensating variation for the price fall. Alternatively the change in the consumer's surplus can be expressed in terms of the higher quantity of X bought rather than by the increase in real income. If the consumer were to buy the same amount of X as he does after the price fall, but have his income reduced to his previous utility, he would be at point F on U_1, so that the distance BF, known as the compensating surplus, is another measure of utility change.

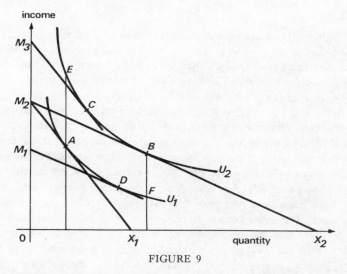

FIGURE 9

Another way to consider the changes in the consumer's utility is in terms of the new rather than the original level. On this basis the substitution effect can be represented by the shift from B to C (where a line parallel to M_2X_1 is tangent to the new utility curve, U_2) and the income effect by AC (a move from U_1 to U_2). In money terms the distance can be measured on the income axis by M_2M_3, known as the equivalent variation for the price fall. Similarly the equivalent surplus, derived from the consumer's original purchases of X but with his income raised to the new level of utility U_2, is the distance AE. Thus there are four measures of the change of surplus which will be identical only in special cases or by coincidence.

These concepts of surplus and variation are useful in providing a theoretical interpretation of how a consumer's utility might be affected by a price change, but the problems inherent in constructing individual indifference curves, let alone aggregating them to assess changes in community utility, are indeed formidable, and in most cases insurmountable. Thus some interpretation in more practicable analytical terms is needed. The most that is likely to be known about an individual's preferences is what he reveals in his demand curve for a particular good, and this includes both income and substitution effects, since income is not normally adjusted to keep utility constant through price changes. Thus the usual curve depicted in economic theory is an 'uncompensated' demand curve, though it is also possible to derive compensated demand curves from diagrams such as Figure 9 above by constructing price–consumption curves along single indifference curves (that is at constant levels of utility). Two such compensated demand lines are shown in Figure 10, in which the positions correspond to those of the same letters in Figure 9, and which can be derived from it via price–consumption curves. Two of the points on the uncompensated demand curve are A and B, positions of consumer equilibrium at prices P_2 and P_1 respectively. The compensated demand curves through A and B (each showing only the substitution effects of a price change) represent levels of utility U_1 and U_2 respectively. Then it can be shown that if the consumer is not compensated

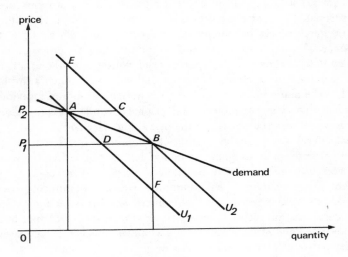

FIGURE 10

for the price change, that is his real income is allowed to rise, the total increase in surplus from the fall in price, including that from the additional real income spent on X, can be represented by P_1P_2AB. (For the derivation of this identity see Winch [1965].) This is equivalent to the Marshallian measure of consumers' surplus, though in this derivation from indifference curves Marshall's cardinal utility assumptions are not necessary. The important aspect of this measure of surplus is that it includes both the income effects (measured in the four ideas of surplus derived from Figure 9) and the substitution effects of buying more of good X because it becomes relatively cheaper. It is the combination of these two factors which the uncompensated demand curve, and its measure of change in consumers' surplus, illustrates.

The idea of surplus has an important application in cost–benefit analysis, where an investment project may lower the price of a product. Other things being equal, this would raise the consumers' surplus of those who originally consumed it and of new consumers who are attracted to the product because it becomes relatively cheaper. This increase may be accounted a benefit to add to the positive side of the calculation. However, it is important to remember that the position of the demand curve is not independent of other considerations, for example the price of other goods and the income of the consumer. So in using consumers' surplus as an adequate measure of each consumer's welfare we are again assuming that these other factors are satisfactory, and in particular that the distribution of income is reasonable so that the prices which consumers are prepared to pay for a good represent adequately their relative utilities from that product. This assumption remains important when we proceed to consider the total consumers' surplus for the market as a whole; this may be considered either as the sum of the individual consumer's surpluses (and as the market demand curve is the horizontal sum of individual's demand curves, market consumers' surplus is similarly represented by the area between the price axis, the prevailing price and the market demand curve), or via the derivation of community indifference curves. In either case some adequate method of aggregating individual welfare is needed to add different consumers' surplus or to construct indifference curves to represent community welfare. Maximising over-all surplus also assumes that total consumers' surplus is the most important consideration rather than adjustments to optimise its distribution between individuals. Comparison of changes which involve losses of utility as well as gains necessitates even stronger assumptions; those incorporated in consumers' surplus may prove to be the most satisfactory, but their implications should be appreciated and acknowledged.

One practical aspect of Marshallian consumers' surplus should be mentioned at this stage, and that is the problems which may arise in its numerical measurement. Accurate knowledge of the demand curve is needed in order to know the maximum price that consumers are willing to pay for each quantity consumed. This knowledge is rarely, if ever, available; all that is usually known is the quantity sold at prevailing prices under present conditions and some idea of the elasticity of demand for small changes in price. To suggest that it is feasible to ascertain the point at which the demand curve meets the price axis and demand is zero is ludicrous for most goods, quite apart from the difficulties of determining the exact position of the demand curve between this point and the present market situation. As an absolute measure of consumers' utility it has virtually insurmountable practical as well as theoretical limitations, but is useful in a situation where maximisation, rather than determination of absolute quantities, is the objective. Its application in both theoretical and policy contexts is discussed further in Chapters 3 and 7.

Genuine attempts to extend Pareto's ideas to assess changes which involve losses for some members of the community have been made by the development of a compensation principle and consumers' surplus, though it is clear that these involve the danger of implicit assumptions which class them as new departures, rather than merely a development, from Paretian principles. There are two further theoretical developments of Pareto's ideas of vital importance which form the subjects of the next two chapters. One is the cautionary tale of comparing non-optimal Paretian situations, which is contained in the General Theory of the Second Best; the other is how we can extend Pareto's comparative-static approach to a more realistic dynamic model.

Suggestions for Further Reading

D. BRAYBROOKE, 'Farewell to the New Welfare Economics', *Review of Economic Studies*, vol. 22 (1954–5).

J. R. HICKS, 'Foundations of Welfare Economics', *Economic Journal*, vol. 49 (1939).

N. KALDOR, 'Welfare Propositions', *Economic Journal*, vol. 49 (1939).

J. R. QUIRK AND R. SAPOSNIK, *General Equilibrium Theory and Welfare Economics* (New York: McGraw-Hill, 1968).

T. SCITOVSKY, 'A Note on Welfare Propositions in Economics', *Review of Economic Studies*, vol. 9 (1941–2).

D. M. WINCH, 'Consumer's Surplus and the Compensation Principle', *American Economic Review*, vol. 55 (1965).

D. M. WINCH, *Analytical Welfare Economics* (Harmondsworth: Penguin, 1971).

Chapter 3

The Second Best

Pareto's principles are designed to show whether or not society is in a position of optimum welfare, and, if not, what are the necessary conditions to reach such an optimum. But suppose that for some reason this ideal position is unattainable and it is known that a Paretian optimum cannot be reached. Is the best policy in these circumstances to fulfil as many of the Paretian conditions as possible in order to get nearly to a Pareto optimum, or does the second-best position lie in an entirely different direction? This controversy was the subject of a paper by Lipsey and Lancaster [1957] which attempted to clarify the general position in such cases; however, before we examine their conclusions in detail, let us consider how relevant the problem of second best is likely to be to practical decision-making.

It cannot be emphasised too strongly that Pareto's criterion for maximum welfare, and the marginal conditions derived from it, were designed as an entire system. Thus Pareto considered not merely the welfare of a particular section of society, or the efficiency of a specific market, but global conditions which would be met throughout the economy, internal and international, when the system as a whole was functioning at maximum efficiency. This, despite its drawbacks (some of which have been mentioned in earlier chapters), was an important start in clarifying the rather vague concepts associated with welfare economics. However, it would be unrealistic to suppose that Paretian conditions for optimum welfare are often likely to be met, and in a case where they are not we have seen that the conditions give no guidance for comparing sub-optimal positions. For example, consider merely one of the Paretian marginal requirements, that the rates of indifferent and technical substitution between all products should be equal. This means, among other things, that all products should be priced such that the ratio of their prices should equal the ratio of their marginal costs, that is, prices equal marginal cost once a *numéraire* has been chosen. Remembering that this condition applies to the whole economy, it therefore requires that all prices should be equal to marginal costs. This will occur under a system of universal perfect competition. Indeed in such a market all Pareto's marginal conditions will be met; but it only requires one imperfection in the market, causing a producer to be faced with a downward-sloping rather than a perfectly elastic demand curve, for the conditions to be violated; for if that producer maximises profits he will put marginal cost equal to marginal revenue, which will be below price, and so the price of the product will exceed marginal cost. Immediately we are faced with a sub-optimal position about which Paretian conditions give no guidance. Indeed such a situation could arise even with perfect private markets if there are externalities of the kind described in Chapter 1, that is the costs with which the producer is faced do not reflect the costs to society as a whole. The discrepancy might arise in either direction – private costs exceed social costs if the producer does some 'good' to society from which he does not himself benefit (for example provides employment in a depressed area without reward) and they will be less than social costs if some harm accrues to society at large for which the producer does not pay (pollution of rivers or air is a typical example). In such a case even if all the marginal conditions are satisfied in the private sense there may not be a Paretian optimum for society as a whole. The Paretian conditions can be amended to encompass such a situation, as was shown in Chapter 1, but in practice the necessary adjustment to bring private and social costs universally into coincidence may not be instituted.

Even more important than these incidental, though very likely, reasons for finding itself in a sub-optimal welfare position is that society itself imposes conditions which preclude maximum efficiency. The most obvious of these is taxation, which in redistributing income within the eonomy is bound to distort to some degree the equality of margins, even if these could be satisfied under *laissez-faire* Government. It was thought for some time that income tax did not distort any such margins, but I. M. D. Little [1957] showed how such a tax affects the margin between work and leisure. In Pareto-optimal circumstances each worker should decide whether and how much to work according to whether his marginal productivity exceeds his marginal valuation of leisure, and will work until these are equal. Even ignoring likely institutional blocks, such as are presented by the existence of standard weeks and trade unions, and assuming that the employer pays each worker his marginal productivity, this will not be the amount received if income tax is imposed, for each employee will cease to work at the point where his net income is equal to his marginal valuation of leisure; if leisure has decreasing marginal utility this means he will work less time than in a Pareto-optimal situation. Basically society has sacrificed one aspect of Paretian efficiency for equity brought about by the redistribution of income through taxation; it is this kind of situation which is represented in Figure 4 (p. 17). The important point to note is that there is a deliberate and virtually universally approved violation of the Paretian optimum in any taxation system which uses marginal taxes, and it does not merely re-adjust for institutional imperfections in the system.

Thus it can be seen that for two basic reasons the over-all Pareto optimum about which there has been so much discussion is unlikely to be achieved in a modern economy. First, it is uncertain whether any perfect market exists in practice, and in any case there are sufficient imperfections throughout industry to result in some substantial departures from the marginal conditions. The Government might be able to mitigate the effect of some of these discrepancies, but could hardly hope to achieve universal equality between the appropriate margins, and even if it could it would not want to, for it deliberately violates the conditions of maximum efficiency in order to satisfy other objectives – such as equity. In practice society judges Pareto's original remit as being incomplete and so adds its own different objectives. In doing so it cannot also expect to aim for a Paretian optimum, for these other considerations automatically make such a position unattainable.

Having established that, in practice, society is virtually certain to be aiming at a second-best, rather than a first-best, position of efficiency, what is known about this 'second-best' situation?

The difficulty lies in the fact that the theory developed in this area has been almost wholly negative, and attempts to establish more positive general conditions have met with little success. In the early 1950s a great deal of attention was given to optimum tariff levels between two or more countries when universal free trade could not be established (that is a second-best efficiency position was the best available), and it was largely as a result of these discussions that Lipsey and Lancaster produced their 'General Theory of the Second Best'. The basic conclusion of their work was that, if any of the Paretian conditions for a first-best welfare position was unavoidably violated, in general the second best could only be obtained by departing from all the other (still attainable) optimum conditions. The proof given with the original theory contained a mathematical error, but this does not affect the general conclusion, and a mathematical statement and corrected proof of the theory can be found in an appendix to this chapter. Thus, in the case of the tariff argument the theory showed that if universal free trade (first best) cannot be achieved, it is better to depart from the other Paretian conditions so that some system of tariffs exists between all countries, rather than abolish tariffs on a piecemeal basis within customs unions. More relevantly for the applications considered in this book, if one industry is not using marginal-cost pricing for some reason (for example as a profit-maximising monopolist) then the second best would require that all other industries also departed from this criterion of first-best Paretian efficiency. We have already established how likely such a diversion from first-best conditions is, so this theory seems to bypass all the carefully constructed arguments of the first two chapters in favour of Paretian optimal conditions.

Indeed the theory of the second best does leave us rather 'high and dry', for not only does it abolish the previously established objectives of first-best conditions, it gives virtually no clue as to where the second-best position is, or even the direction of departure from first-best criteria necessary to maximise the chance of achieving the second best — it merely informs us of where the second best is not (namely achieving all first-best criteria possible). Several attempts have been made since the Theory of the Second Best was published to establish more positively its position relative to that of the first best, but few of these are of much practical interest since the assumptions needed to obtain a workable model render the results extremely restrictive. However, it is interesting to consider some of these ideas.

The first was produced by Lipsey and Lancaster in their original statement of the second-best theory. They examined various examples of the application of the theory, one of which involved a three-industry economy, including a profit-maximising monopolist and a nationalised industry whose pricing policy was to be used by the Government to aim for maximum achievable (that is second-best) welfare. Interesting as this proved in terms of mathematical modelling of such an economy, the assumptions made about the relation of production costs and demand between the products render the resulting conclusions too restrictive for generalisation in a practical situation. Further development along the lines of mathematical model-building of particular second-best situations was attempted by H. A. J. Green [1961], who developed the second-order conditions necessary for the existence of a second-best welfare position. As can be imagined from the first-order conditions developed in the appendix, these second-best conditions are complex (much more so than for a Paretian optimum) and do not lend themselves readily to economic interpretation. Again, Green tried to deduce conditions for particular second-best situations, and some discussion of his work followed, but as in the original article the result is more relevant as an example of a mathematical model than as a guide to practical policy decisions.

A different approach to locating the second-best welfare position was followed by Ralph Turvey in his book *Optimal Pricing and Investment in Electricity Supply* [1968] which took a more pragmatic view of a particular problem, the optimal level of electricity prices in a situation constrained by prices unequal to marginal costs in other industries. He suggested that if the producers of a close substitute priced above marginal cost then so should the industry concerned, while it should follow the reverse policy if prices of close complements, inputs in production or products for which this industry's goods are an input, are above marginal cost. This argument was based on ensuring that the final allocation of demand within a sector is as close as possible to that which would exist in a first-best situation, that is one of universal marginal-cost pricing. (We are assuming here of course that other marginal conditions, such as that payment to factors equals their marginal productivity, are also satisfactory.) The Turvey criteria seem intuitively sensible, and in many cases may prove to be the most practical guide, particularly for largely 'self-sufficient' sectors of industry such as fuel and transport, but its limitations should also be realised.

The chief of these arises in the precise definitions of a 'complement', for all goods are substitutes in the sense that they compete for the consumer's income, while some clearly also complement each other in consumption. Perhaps the best way to illustrate this is with an example from the electricity industry itself, where clearly the purchase of a washing machine and the electricity with which to operate it are complementary. Yet the sacrifice of income necessary to obtain the machine may be so great that economies must be made in, say, the use of electricity for central heating. Thus the washing machine and electricity can be both complements and substitutes in consumption. Similarly electricity and gas are thought of as substitutes but become complements in a gas central-heating system with an electrically operated clock and pump (as the owners of such systems discover to their irritation when the electricity supply ceases). Thus the definition of complements and substitutes may not be as straightforward as first appears. Another practical problem arises in determining just how widely divergences from marginal cost should be taken into account. It has already been emphasised that all products are substitutes to the consumer, because all represent alternative ways of spending his income. Should we therefore attempt to include the whole gamut of consumer products and their divergences from marginal cost in assessing what Government policy should be? Clearly this would enlarge the scope of the problem so far as to make it intractable; but deciding just where the line should be drawn is not easy. Should we consider the woollen-garment industry in studies of fuel prices for example, or the bicycle industry in transport policy, where clearly some tenuous connections exist? There can be no hard-and-fast rule in such cases, though in practice the limits must be drawn fairly narrowly because of limited information and the need to obtain some answer reasonably quickly. Despite its theoretical limitations Turvey's *ad hoc* approach may provide the most feasible guidelines for second-best policy.

While considering the second best it may be worth mentioning a common misunderstanding about pricing policy, particularly prevalent in the early discussions of second best. This was that if one industry was digressing from marginal-cost pricing, the optimum would be restored if all other industries put their prices in the same ratio to marginal costs, in other words proportionality between prices and marginal costs is all that is required. The fallacy arises because this proportionality must hold for all goods and factors throughout the economy, so its only effect is to change the basic *numéraire* which defines the value of money, and to bring prices and marginal costs back into equality. This may be a useful accounting technique in the unlikely event that there is only one 'rogue' industry over which the Government has no control, but in economic terms this solution is either incomplete because it cannot be applied to all industries, or it is meaningless because it brings the economy back to a first-best situation in which marginal equality exists.

However, there is an argument for marginal-cost pricing which avoids the second-best issue by concentrating on welfare only within a particular industry, and not for the community as a whole. In this situation there is no need to consider explicitly imperfections in other industries since these will be reflected automatically in the demand and cost curves of the sector under consideration. The objective of this model is to maximise total market surplus, that is the sum of consumers' and producers' surplus, and takes no account of the distribution of this total. In practice it may be very important that a particular section of consumers receives a significant level of surplus (for example in the fuel industries emphasis is often laid on the needs of poor and elderly consumers), but the maximisation of total surplus is a particularly attractive criterion for nationalised industries in which the productive unit is owned communally. For with Government control over production a producer's loss need not result in bankruptcy, and redistribution of surplus between producer and consumers and within the consuming group is possible through subsidies and taxes.

The concept of consumers' surplus has been defined in the previous chapter and producers' profits and losses can be considered in similar terms. A producer's surplus is defined as the difference between the minimum price a producer would be willing to accept at each quantity supplied and the price the market offers him. For a profit-maximising producer facing given market prices, the minimum price at which he would be prepared to supply would be his marginal cost, and so for each unit sold his surplus is equal to the difference between price and marginal cost. Note that this may be negative for some units whose marginal cost exceeds price (see Figure 11).

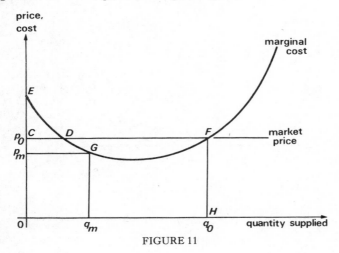

FIGURE 11

A profit-maximising producer selling quantity q_o at price p_o has a producer's surplus of $p_o - p_M$ on the q_Mth unit ($q_M < q_o$), and for all units between D and F the producer's surplus will be represented by the area $DGFD$. However, between C and D there is producer loss represented at each unit by the extent to which marginal cost exceeds p_o. Thus the total producer surplus is equal to $DGFD - CDEC$. This is merely the profit made by the producer since total revenue is equal to $0CFH$ and the total cost is represented by the area under the marginal-cost curve (since marginal cost is the differential of total cost), that is $EC0HFGDE$. Producers' surplus is therefore represented by the area between selling price and the marginal-cost curve.

The concepts of consumers' and producers' surplus can be combined to consider total market surplus and its maximisation. Three possible price levels are shown in Figures 12, 13 and 14: price below, equal to, and above, marginal cost. When price is below marginal cost, as shown in Figure 12, total consumer surplus is equal to $ACBA$, and net producer surplus is represented by $DGFD$ minus $ECDE$ and $FBQHF$. Thus total net surplus is the area enclosed by the demand and marginal-cost curves less the triangle $HBQH$, since the other areas of producer loss are cancelled by consumers' surplus. When price equals marginal cost (Figure 13) there is no uncancelled part of producer loss, and total market surplus is represented by the area $AEKGHA$. However, if price rises above marginal cost (Figure 14) the consumers' surplus contracts to the area $ALMNA$, so total net

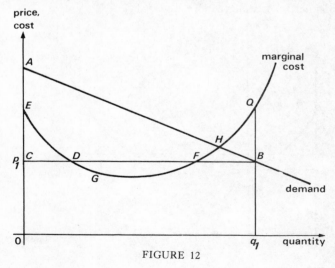

FIGURE 12

producer and consumer surplus is shown by *AEMGSNA*. It is clear from these diagrams that total market surplus is at a maximum when price equals marginal cost, that is at level p_M.

How does this single-market argument for one of Pareto's marginal conditions fit in with the second-best principle for the economy as a

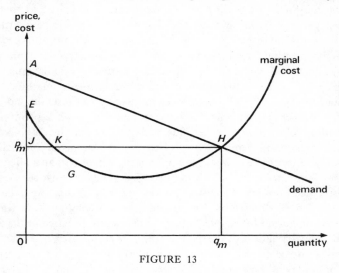

FIGURE 13

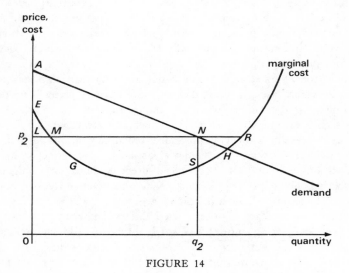

FIGURE 14

whole? Despite the analysis of only one market, influences elsewhere in the economy are not neglected since these are reflected in the demand and cost curves of the market under consideration. For example, if there are heavy subsidies to the railway industry, this is bound to affect demand for road transport, and so the price and quantity at which marginal-cost pricing will bring about equilibrium in that industry will depend on railway policy. In general, if a close substitute is priced below marginal cost, this will shift the demand curve down from the position in which universal marginal-cost pricing prevails, and so marginal-cost pricing within the industry would result in a lower price than if the whole economy were using marginal-cost pricing. But it will still be marginal-cost pricing so far as the industry itself is concerned, and the objective in following such a policy is to maximise its own market surplus and not to aim for a universal welfare maximum. Similarly it will take costs 'as given', and these, too, may reflect distortions in other markets which will also affect the marginal-cost price, but which in maximising only its own surplus the industry need not consider. It is interesting to note that this policy is likely to lead to diversions from the first-best pricing position similar to those suggested by Ralph Turvey as deliberate practice in the electricity industry. For if the price of an input is above marginal cost, this will raise the costs of the electricity industry and so private marginal-cost pricing would result in higher electricity prices than in a Paretian-optimum system. To deliberately price above private marginal costs would involve pushing prices even higher, and it is not clear whether Turvey was suggesting such a policy. Indeed, maximising market surplus would automatically involve diversions of the sort which Turvey recommended, except for the adjustment necessary if prices of products for which electricity is a major input diverge from marginal costs, in which case a deliberate change in electricity prices is needed. Although, like the Turvey argument, the maximisation of market surplus seems a somewhat *ad hoc* approach, its attraction lies in the frequent necessity to provide piecemeal recommendations for public-sector industries. Indeed it becomes a particularly attractive argument for such industries which are given no direct guidance, or ambiguous instructions about pricing policies − which in practice frequently occurs. They seem to have a justifiable argument that their concern is only with the welfare of their own industry and that this implies marginal-cost pricing. Indeed it is worth noting that the argument still holds in this context even if it involves a producer loss, that is if average cost is above marginal cost (see Figure 15). In this case total surplus is still maximum at price p_M and is equal to *AFDEA*, although the producer has a net loss represented by *FCDF*. In particular, in the case of average-cost pricing, which is often recommended to avoid losses in such decreasing-cost industries, the total net surplus will be *AFGHEA*, which is less than if price is set equal to marginal cost. Thus marginal private cost pricing will maximise total net surplus for each industry, though it may result in a producer loss and uneven distribution of consumers' surplus.

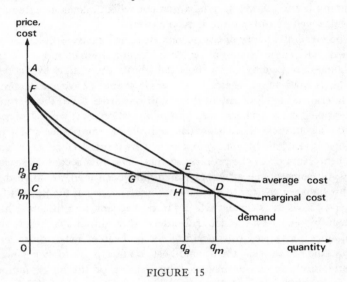

FIGURE 15

One other theoretical argument in favour of marginal-cost pricing in the public sector has been promoted, largely by French economists and engineers concerned with electricity tariffs (Nelson [1964]). This is basically a 'common-sense' approach which also appears at first to involve only one industry. The argument is that an individual can only choose sensibly whether to consume an extra unit of, say, electricity, by comparing the cost of that unit (marginal cost) with the satisfaction he will receive from it (marginal utility). A utility-maximising consumer will buy goods such that the ratio of the prices is equal to the ratio of his marginal utilities and so marginal-cost pricing ensures that the marginal-utilities/marginal-cost ratio is the same for all goods. Thus, in maximising his own utility, the consumer faced with marginal-cost electricity prices will buy that amount of electricity which brings equality between the consumer's marginal utility and marginal cost to society, and will so help to achieve the optimum allocation of resources. This argument is basically a verbal expression of the ideas which Pareto's criteria state more formally, and a brief consideration shows that the argument only holds if *all* prices are equal to marginal cost, since otherwise the marginal-utility/marginal-cost ratios will be distorted, and like Pareto's system it gives no guidance to the position of the second best. Indeed the only case for marginal-cost pricing which withstands distortions elsewhere in the economy is the market-surplus argument which makes no attempt to consider welfare outside the industry itself.

The General Theory of the Second Best, as its name implies, is concerned with any violation of Pareto's conditions, and of course marginal-cost pricing, on which the above discussion has concentrated, is only one of these. However, it should be clear that similar considerations apply if any of the conditions are broken; the marginal-cost-pricing case has been used as an illustration, partly because much of the second-best discussion has centred on this issue, and partly because it is a controversial public policy area. It therefore serves as an excellent example of the problems which arise in a second-best situation, and some of the attempts which have been made to solve them. In this light we can try to view the General Theory of the Second Best in perspective. It is certainly likely to be relevant, and therefore has a devastating effect on the neat rules derived to aim at a first-best solution, since these are no longer directly applicable. Yet it gives us no useful guide as to what the second-best conditions are; only pragmatic criteria, such as those suggested by Turvey or the single-industry market-surplus maximisation principle, can be applied. The main value of Lipsey and Lancaster's theory may thus be in encouraging general scepticism about 'easy answers' to problems of economic policy, particularly when these are based on glib recommendations of marginal criteria rather than in providing constructive alternatives. It should also be remembered that all the discussion has so far been in terms only of economic efficiency, and a diversion from Pareto's conditions may be not only inevitable, but also desirable for the fulfilment of other economic and social objectives. Just how these various criteria can be moulded into practical policy is discussed in Part Two.

Appendix to Chapter 3: General Theory of the Second Best – Statement and Proof

Lipsey and Lancaster [1957] consider a function $F(x_1, x_2, \ldots, x_n)$ of the n variables $x_1, x_2, \ldots, x_n$, where F is a utility function and x_i is the quantity of commodity i which is consumed. F is to be maximised (minimised) subject to a constraint $\phi(x_1, \ldots, x_n) = 0$ (ϕ being a production-possibilities restraint). They suppose that the solution to this problem, that is the Paretian optimum, is the $n-1$ equations Ω^i $(x_1, \ldots, x_n) = 0$, for $i = 1, 2, \ldots, n-1$. The theorem of the second best is stated as follows. If there is an additional constraint imposed of the type $\Omega^i \neq 0$ for $i = j$, then the maximum (minimum) of F subject to both the constraint ϕ and the constraint $\Omega^i \neq 0$ will, in general, be such that none of the still attainable Paretian conditions, $\Omega^i = 0$, $i \neq j$, will be satisfied.

PROOF

Using Lagrange multipliers to find the Paretian optimum we have

$$F_i - \lambda \phi_i = 0, \qquad i = 1, 2, \ldots, n, \tag{1}$$

which can be expressed as

$$\frac{F_i}{F_n} = \frac{\phi_i}{\phi_n}, \qquad i = 1, 2, \ldots, n-1, \tag{2}$$

where the nth commodity is chosen as the *numéraire*.

Now suppose a constraint is imposed which prevents the attainment of one of the conditions, say

$$\frac{F_l}{F_n} = k \frac{\phi_l}{\phi_n}, \qquad k \neq 1. \tag{3}$$

Since there is an additional constraint the function now to be maximised (minimised) is

$$F - \lambda' \phi - \mu \left\{ \frac{F_l}{F_n} - k \frac{\phi_l}{\phi_n} \right\}, \tag{4}$$

where λ', μ are Lagrange constants.

The condition for this expression to be maximised (minimised) is as follows:

$$F_i - \lambda' \phi_i - \mu \left\{ \frac{F_n F_{li} - F_l F_{ni}}{F_n^2} - k \frac{\phi_n \phi_{li} - \phi_l \phi_{ni}}{\phi_n^2} \right\} = 0,$$

$$i = 1, 2, \ldots, n. \tag{5}$$

Let

$$\frac{F_n F_{li} - F_l F_{ni}}{F_n^2} = Q_i$$

and

$$\frac{\phi_n \phi_{li} - \phi_l \phi_{ni}}{\phi_n^2} = R_i.$$

Then

$$F_i = \lambda' \phi_i + \mu(Q_i - kR_i)$$

$$\frac{F_i}{F_n} = \frac{\lambda' \phi_i + \mu(Q_i - kR_i)}{\lambda' \phi_n + \mu(Q_n - kR_n)}$$

$$= \frac{\phi_i + \frac{\mu}{\lambda'}(Q_i - kR_i)}{\phi_n + \frac{\mu}{\lambda'}(Q_n - kR_n)}. \tag{6}$$

This is the condition of the second-best position given the constraint (3) and is not the condition which Lipsey and Lancaster quote in equation 7(6) of their paper which is

$$\frac{F_i}{F_n} = \frac{\phi_i}{\phi_n} \left[\frac{1 + \frac{\mu}{\lambda'}(Q_i - kR_i)}{1 + \frac{\mu}{\lambda'}(Q_n - kR_n)} \right].$$

Up to the derivation of this equation their method is accurate, but the conditions which they conclude occur in specific instances, based on their version of equation (6), are incorrect. However, it should be noted that this does not in any way upset their *general* conclusions.

Applying Lipsey and Lancaster's methods to equation (6), it can be seen that any one of these conditions for the second best is the same as the equivalent Paretian condition if and only if

$$\frac{\phi_i + \frac{\mu}{\lambda'}(Q_i - kR_i)}{\phi_n + \frac{\mu}{\lambda'}(Q_n - kR_n)} = \frac{\phi_i}{\phi_n},$$

that is

$$\phi_n\phi_i + \phi_n\frac{\mu}{\lambda'}(Q_i - kR_i) = \phi_i\phi_n + \phi_i\frac{\mu}{\lambda'}(Q_n - kR_n),$$

that is

$$\frac{\phi_i}{\phi_n} = \frac{Q_i - kR_i}{Q_n - kR_n},$$

or

$$\frac{\phi_i}{\phi_n} = \frac{\left\{\dfrac{F_i}{F_n} - k\dfrac{\phi_i}{\phi_n}\right\}_i}{\left\{\dfrac{F_i}{F_n} - k\dfrac{\phi_i}{\phi_n}\right\}_n}. \tag{7}$$

Lipsey and Lancaster's version is

$$\frac{1 + \dfrac{\mu}{\lambda'}(Q_i - kR_i)}{1 + \dfrac{\mu}{\lambda'}(Q_n - kR_n)} = 1.$$

In general there is no reason to suppose that the equality (7) holds and so a departure from Paretian conditions is indeed necessary to achieve a second-best position.

Suggestions for Further Reading

R. G. LIPSEY AND R. K. LANCASTER, 'The General Theory of the Second Best', *Review of Economic Studies*, vol. 24 (1957).

M. McMANUS, 'Comments on the General Theory of the Second Best', *Review of Economic Studies*, vol. 26 (1959).

RALPH TURVEY, *Optimal Pricing and Investment in Electricity Supply* (London: Allen & Unwin, 1968).

Chapter 4

Efficiency in a Dynamic Economy

So far the discussion of Paretian efficiency conditions has been in terms of a static economy, that is one in which the problem is to maximise welfare by the distribution of a given number of resources. In practice the stock of resources can be used at different rates and in different ways to give various output totals and mixes at different points in time. This chapter is concerned with the principles and problems of extending Paretian criteria to this more realistic situation.

In theory the markets which deal in the relation of output at various points in time are similar to any other economic markets, and are places where those who wish to trade consumption now for consumption later can meet, and strike a bargain with, those who prefer to borrow against future earnings. The market thus acts merely as an intermediary between a large number of people who express their preferences in the price they are willing to accept or pay for money, and in a perfectly competitive situation a single price for any particular type of borrowing or lending should prevail (it is normally assumed that preferences result in a premium being paid to borrow for present consumption against future repayments). Since the marginal utility of consumption decreases in any one time period we would expect the usual shaped indifference curve, that is convex to the origin,

and at each prevailing rate of interest (shown b
market rate-of-exchange curve), the consumer w
total utility by reaching the highest possible ind
would be in *n* dimensions for *n* time periods, bv
principle by a two-dimensional diagram repre..
now and consumption next year (see Figure 16). 'I ..
maximises his utility at *C* by allocating resources so that the ra..
exchange between present and future consumption in the market is
equal to his own valuation of the relative worth of these amounts. This
position and the amount of income available to him now and in the
future will determine his net borrowing or lending in the market. Thus
we have essentially established an additional 'dynamic' Paretian condition for maximising consumer welfare.

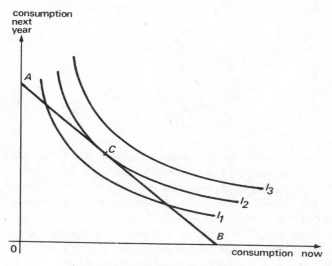

C is the consumption yielding maximum utility

The slope of *AB* represents the market rate of interest

The distance of the line *AB* from the origin represents the total available income

FIGURE 16

However, there is another aspect which influences supply and demand in the money markets, namely the technical possibilities for investment, or converting assets now into future returns. If we again
assume the classic relation between outputs, and regard an investment

.ve through time as a special case of a production-possibility curve,
ie surface will be concave to the origin if there are limited
possibilities for investment in any one time period. Again the two-
dimensional case can be illustrated as in Figure 17.

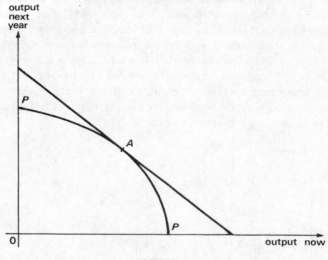

FIGURE 17

The production-possibility curve *PP* shows the combinations of
total output in each time period which can be achieved using a given
level of resources, and the producer maximises his return at the point
where the rate of exchange in production is equal to the rate of
exchange in the market, that is point *A* on production-possibility curve
PP. Thus in production, too, a 'dynamic' condition can be added to
those necessary for a Paretian optimum, and this will determine
whether the producer lends or borrows in the market. In a perfectly
competitive market we would expect all producers and consumers to
lend and borrow exactly that amount which maximised the welfare of
each, and this would establish a single market rate of equilibrium.
This situation can be represented by a 'universal' production-
possibility curve between two years showing an amalgam of all
producers' available investment opportunities, and a series of indifference curves combining all individuals' preferences about consumption now and in the future (see Figure 18). (The practical
problems of constructing such curves are virtually insurmountable, but
this does not detract from their use as a theoretical explanation.) The

point of equilibrium will be where each consumer has the same rate of exchange between the time periods as is represented by the opportunities available and shown by the slope of the production curve. Since one rate of interest exists this can also be said to represent the trade-off between consumption in different time periods for the whole community, and would exist at point C in Figure 18. The slope of the line at this point represents the unique rate of interest established by

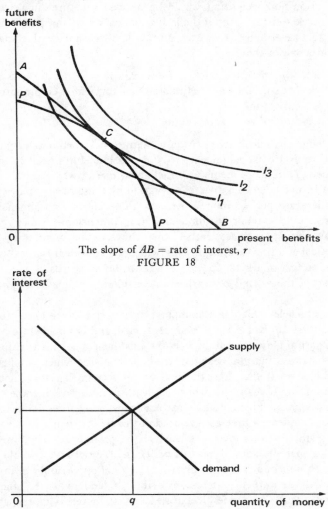

The slope of AB = rate of interest, r

FIGURE 18

FIGURE 19

the supply of, and demand for, money (r in Figure 19), and at the margin all borrowers and lenders have the same rate of exchange between present and future benefits, thus satisfying the 'extended Pareto' conditions.

The above explanation does oversimplify some aspects of the analysis, particularly that of deriving a community indifference curve from individual preferences. Clearly some assumptions about income distribution and weighting would be necessary before such a curve could be established, even if the individual curves themselves could be accurately ascertained. However, all that is important for this analysis is an acceptance that

(a) individual indifference curves do exist;

(b) they can be meaningfully combined to yield a community in-difference curve; and

(c) they are convex to the origin.

Knowledge of their exact position or nature will (fortunately!) not be needed; only their general pattern and possible shifts need to be es-tablished. Thus there seems in principle no reason why Pareto's ideas cannot be extended to a dynamic situation by these means, particular-ly if there are perfect money markets. (The above two-dimensional analysis can be extended to three and more dimensions for many years by considering surfaces rather than lines.) The problems, both theoretical and practical, begin only when one considers the real world where perfect markets do not exist; in other words a particular problem of the second best arises in considering policy in a dynamic situation.

The obstacle which is the main cause of the divergence from a Pareto optimum has already been mentioned, and is a deliberate policy on the part of Government, namely the existence of income tax. Just as it distorts the margin between work and leisure when applied to earned income, it also alters the relation between gross returns and net receipts from investment when applied to unearned income. The problem is in practice a double one, for taxes are charged twice on in-vestment returns — first as corporation tax to the firm receiving the returns and again as income tax when the profits are distributed to stock- or share-holders. What in a perfect market situation would be a unique equilibrium rate of return (the marginal opportunity of invest-ment and the rate of interest available to lenders in the market) becomes two, often widely separated, rates. In terms of the above analysis the existence of taxation reduces the net future amount a company can hope to receive for any given present investment, and has the same effect on lenders. Thus, for any given level of technical investment opportunities available to society, investors will actually receive a lower rate of return, and the new 'highest' indifference curve that can be reached (I_1) is not tangent to, but cuts, the production-possibility curve at B, and is less steep at its point of contact than the common tangent in a perfect market (Figure 20). In terms of supply

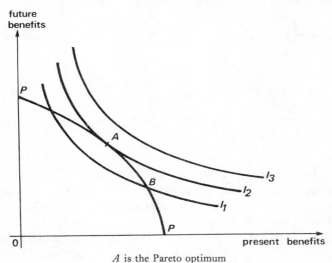

A is the Pareto optimum

B is market equilibrium in the presence of taxation

The slope of I_1 at B represents the net return to investors

The slope of PP at B represents the gross return to companies

FIGURE 20

and demand analysis the existence of taxation shifts both curves; the relation of the over-all equilibrium rate of interest after tax to that which would exist in a 'free market' is impossible to determine without detailed knowledge of tax rates and supply and demand elasticities. (Figure 21 shows the *directions* in which the curves shift.) It can be seen from this discussion that taxation will constrain the equilibrium position in the money markets away from the Pareto optimum, and remove the neat single rate of interest which would prevail in free and perfect markets. However, such taxation is virtually inevitable, and perhaps desirable, in a modern economy, so economists are faced with identifying the second-best position.

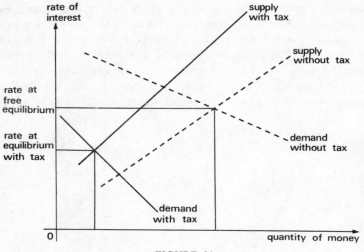

FIGURE 21

It may be appropriate here to anticipate some of the contents of later chapters in explaining the practical importance of such an apparently abstract discussion on interest rates. Many Government decisions involve the best use of resources over time, both in terms of investment and consumption. We shall see this clearly in the examples used in Parts Two and Three later in this book. Correct public-sector investment decisions, the use of cost–benefit analysis, and decisions on the depletion of natural resources, all require some means of relating the worth of future benefits and sacrifices to those met at the present. This can clearly only be achieved by using some rate of discount, not necessarily the same for each year, but usually assumed to be positive, by which present and future experiences can be related. If a free market with a unique rate of interest were in operation, this single rate, which represents opportunities and demand patterns of all members of the community, would be the obvious choice for the rate of discount. But we now have at least two clear candidates: that which members of the community receive, and which represents the rate of interest at which their lending and borrowing is in equilibrium, and the higher rate available as gross return on marginal investment in private industry. As an alternative some might suggest the use of an intermediate figure, or that rate which would exist in free markets – if this could be ascertained. None of these rates is obviously better for discounting than any other.

Although it is only necessary to establish for the purpose of this discussion in principle that a unique rate of interest does not exist, and the most important reason for this is the imposition of taxation, there are two other factors which tend to disturb the equilibrium of money markets and which often lead to fluctuating rates of interest. The first is also the result of direct Government influence, namely deliberate interference in the money markets to further other social or economic ends. Recently the most common influence has been to encourage high interest rates and attract foreign funds to London to safeguard our external balance, but low-interest policies have also been followed to stimulate consumer spending and industrial investment. Although the markets used for these policies have usually been those dealing with short-term loans, there have been repurcussions in all money markets. Interest rates may vary between markets for different lengths and security of loan, and it is usually the long-term market which is relevant for Government discount rates since this reflects best the types of investment undertaken in the public sector. Nevertheless the interaction between the different money markets causes interference in short-term interest rates to be reflected in the equilibrium rate of interest for long-term loans.

A particular form of uncertainty which may cause fluctuations in the money markets is inflation, and many of the applications mentioned later are concerned with the accurate prediction and control of this variable. Clearly it is desirable that both private and public decisions should be based on real returns and costs, but even if *money* returns are certain, differing views about the rate of inflation may make unanimity about real values difficult to achieve; the problem may be further complicated if the use of particular inflation forecasts in a Government study becomes a political issue. This factor may prevent a unique equilibrium being reached even in the absence of other distortions, and can cause considerable fluctuations in both the real and money rates of interest exhibited in the market.

Having ascertained that, for a variety of reasons, no unique long-term interest rate is likely to prevail, can we develop some principle to determine the rate of discount for public policy decisions, and decide whether a unique rate of discount for each year, or different rates in different circumstances, are more appropriate? One argument favours the use of the net receipts of long-term investors as the discount rate; its proponents argue that this is the rate at which borrowers and lenders (and those who do not enter the money markets) are in equilibrium, and this rate therefore represents the marginal valuation of future benefits in terms of present income for each individual in the community. It is therefore the most appropriate rate for the Government to use in discounting for the whole community. This argument implies that each individual will indeed invest or borrow such that his rate of exchange between present and future benefits is equal to that available in the market; it ignores, among other things, any fixed costs of entering the market or discontinuities in lending or borrowing opportunities which may prevent such equality between margins from being achieved. In practice of course there are such institutional imperfections in the market, but it is difficult to know how best to adjust for them, and in principle at least the use of the 'net receipts rate' does seem to reflect consumers' preferences.

However, if the Government does use such a rate to judge public-sector projects, the distortion between gross returns to companies and net receipts by individuals becomes relevant. For if the test discount rate based on receipts is, say, 5 per cent per annum in real terms, this may represent a gross return on private-investment projects of about 12 per cent (assuming corporation tax of 40 per cent and personal tax of 35 per cent). Thus to use a rate of 5 per cent to assess public-sector projects when a 12 per cent return is available on marginal investment projects in the private sector would divert resources to the public sector which could earn a higher return in private industry.

(The figures used above are fairly arbitrary – it seems highly unlikely that a real net return approaching 5 per cent has been available to investors recently, and not all consumers face a marginal tax rate of 33 per cent. Similarly, it is difficult to determine the real rate of taxation paid on profits; investment grants and tax concessions may lower taxation rates, but the practice of historic-cost depreciation is likely to result in an under-estimate of true costs, an over-estimate of profits and hence a higher tax rate on real profits. But the principle remains that discounting at the net rate available in the market must cause considerable discrepancy between the public and private sectors.)

Perhaps, then, it would be better to use the marginal private opportunity rate of discount for the public sector, so that funds are directed to public or private projects according to where potential returns are highest. The problem here is that discounting at a rate much higher than the net return to investors would involve abandoning many projects whose net benefits would be valued as positive by consumers who discount at the market rate. Thus we seem to be caught between two alternatives – to get the balance between public and private sectors correct or to balance society's valuation of the present and future

– while using either must cause distortion in the other criterion.

A number of compromises have been suggested to overcome this dilemma. One is that the private opportunity cost of capital should be used to discount costs and returns which would otherwise be used in the private sector, and the net market return (also often called the social time preference rate or S.T.P.R.) should be used for discounting costs and benefits whose alternative destination is consumption (see, for example, Feldstein [1964]). In principle this idea is attractive, but in practice the alternative use of Government income is very difficult to determine, since virtually all funds are channelled through the Treasury which may collect extra money by reducing consumption via taxation or cutting investment grants to industry, or rationing other public-sector projects. So, adequate as this 'mix' of rates might be in theory, it cannot usually be used as a practical compromise because the necessary information is not available.

There is no 'right' answer to the best discount rate to use in general; distortions in the market, and the two resulting candidates, leave us with a second-best dilemma which, like most such problems, does not lend itself to a ready solution. Probably, for most projects which involve a mix of consumption and investment sources of costs and destinations of benefits, the application of each rate to the appropriate parts of the equation would result in an equivalent single rate somewhere between the two individual rates used. (This is not invariably so, particularly if the project involves a period of net benefits sandwiched between initial net investment costs and subsequent net 'clear-up' costs, but is true for most typical investment projects.) This may suggest that a single compromise rate could be used somewhere between the marginal private opportunity rate and the social time preference rate. For most purposes this is probably the best that Government can hope for, even though it will probably involve distortions in both dimensions by using neither rate. This is not, incidentally, the argument which Governments have used in practice when suggesting discount rates for use in public-sector projects, as we shall see in later chapters.

However, there are circumstances in which one of the two rates appears much more appropriate than the other. For example, if the Government has a fixed amount of money which it is considering for use either in a private- or public-investment project, and the receipts from each will be equally liable to tax, then not to use the private opportunity rate to discount both projects would give an obviously biased result. (In this case the funds are not being considered for consumption so the social time preference rate is not relevant.) Even more important is the converse case when private investment is irrelevant, for a decision on timing of consumption alone must be made, and the problem is merely one of comparing the net worth of different consumption patterns. Here it is clearly the social time preference rate which should be used to discount, and this is an important consideration in determining the optimal rate of depleting natural resources, a problem which has recently aroused considerable public interest. Some practical implications of using the social time preference rate in such circumstances will emerge later, particularly in Chapter 10.

The discussion has centred on *the* rate of discount as if only one rate applies to all future years, whereas in principle there is no reason why it should not vary, perhaps be 5 per cent per annum for five years and then rise or fall for subsequent years to reflect changes in expected standards of living or merely the tastes of the community in different time spans. However, in practice the problem of establishing even some average figure appropriate for discounting is so fraught with difficulties that few economists reach the stage of discussing the fluctuations over time. We, too, shall confine ourselves to the consideration of a single rate, though not with any prejudice against the idea that this may reflect a number of discount rates for different years.

The problem of determining discount rates has been discussed at some length, for it illustrates two important aspects of welfare economics, the problem of determining what is the best course in principle and of converting that principle to practical guidelines; and as we shall see later it is a problem which is extremely important in its implications for Government policy. Many of the points suggested here will be developed in Chapter 6 on investment policy, to which these principles have direct application, but the problems involved will return at various points throughout the rest of the book.

Suggestions for Further Reading

K. J. ARROW, 'Discounting and Public Investment Criteria', in *Water Resources Research,* ed. A. V. Kneese and S. C. Smith (Baltimore: Johns Hopkins Press, 1966).

M. S. FELDSTEIN, 'Net Social Benefits and the Public Investment Decision', *Oxford Economic Papers,* vol. 16 (1964).

M. S. FELDSTEIN AND J. M. FLEMING, 'The Problem of Time-Stream Evaluation: Present Value versus Internal Rate of Return Rules',

Bulletin of the Oxford University Institute of Economics and Statistics, vol. 26 (1964).

S. A. MARGLIN, 'The Social Rate of Discount and the Optimum Rate of Investment', *Quarterly Journal of Economics*, vol. 77 (1963).

E. J. MISHAN, *Elements of Cost Benefit Analysis* (London: Allen & Unwin, 1972).

Chapter 5

Assessment of Neoclassical Welfare Economics

This seems an appropriate place to assess how far the theories presented in the first four chapters provide a useful guide to economic policy. The Paretian conditions described in Chapter 1 yielded some criteria for welfare judgements, even though their basis is rather narrow; they can be extended using a compensation principle, but this involves substantial distributional judgements. An even greater drawback in practice is the lack of guidance provided by Pareto's theory for the second-best situation, which forms the background for most economic decisions. These considerations do not create an encouraging impression for theorist or practitioner in the field of welfare economics, and it may be helpful to try and assess the arguments in a wider context.

First there is the question of how far efficiency alone should be the guide for policy decisions. Most citizens would agree that there are many other criteria for the welfare of the community which should bear at least some emphasis. The most obvious is that the way in which the economic 'cake' is distributed is almost as important as the total size of the cake (it is the latter which Paretian conditions seek to maximise). However, the exact emphasis to be placed on distribution and size is a matter of political debate, and even if some mutually

agreeable balance between these factors, and all the others which
affect economic welfare, could be achieved, we cannot at present
analyse them comprehensively to yield useful policy guidelines
(though, as Chapter 8 shows, cost–benefit analysis is one development
in this direction). This may seem a very negative argument for returning to the consideration of efficiency criteria alone, but when faced
with the choice between using what he knows to be an inefficient and
incomplete instrument, and abandoning the problem because of its
complexity, the economist may reluctantly follow the former course,
albeit aware of the limitations inherent in the analysis. Hence despite
recognition that it is not the only, or even necessarily the most important, factor in social welfare, economists continue to concentrate on
the maximisation of economic efficiency.

The obvious place to start such a study is to look at the best position which can be reached (and this is what Pareto did), establishing
conditions which defined the position of greatest efficiency. Some of
these need re-interpretation in particular circumstances where the
definition of the appropriate marginal rate is unclear, but apart from
one or two theoretical anomalies they provide unambiguous criteria to
judge efficiency. Problems in using them arise when the change under
discussion does not obey Pareto's strict rules for improved welfare,
and when constraints on the economy prevent the first-best position
from being attained. It is the converse of the clear conditions for
maximum welfare which Pareto provides that they are not applicable
in part, and in these situations provide no guideline at all as to the optimum policy. It is interesting to note that many members of the
public seem unaware of the limitations of Pareto's conditions. They
have a vague idea that competition is a 'good thing' because they
recollect that it can sometimes lead to maximum efficiency, and this
may even suggest to them that free enterprise should therefore be sup-
ported in all forms so that the economy can 'automatically' adjust to
an optimum position. Right-wing politicians are notoriously prone to
believe this fallacy. It is worth emphasising at this stage that although
there are circumstances in which this argument holds it will not do so
on Paretian grounds if either:

(*a*) there is not perfect competition in the industries concerned, for
profit maximisation will not result in the establishment of Paretian
marginal conditions; or

(*b*) these marginal conditions do not hold at all other points in the
economy, for in this case a first-best position is unattainable and
Pareto's criteria are irrelevant.

These two stumbling blocks to the efficiency of free enterprise in any particular industry are likely to exist in the vast majority of cases. Since in practice it will always be a 'second-best' optimum which is the objective we may feel justified in turning hopefully to the 'General Theory of the Second Best' for guidance.

However, all this does is to underline the inadequacy of a partial approach by proving that the second-best optimum involves, in general, departure from even the still-attainable Paretian marginal conditions. Attempts to define more positively the second-best position have resulted either in economic models too restrictive to provide significant practical guidance or mathematical expressions too complicated to lend themselves to economic interpretation. The second-best theory may tempt us to abandon even the analysis of efficiency since there are no positive guidelines if the optimum is unattainable.

Despite these discouragements some progress in analysing welfare problems can and should be made. To abandon a problem because it seems intractable, and recommend that Governments choose economic policies at random or 'intuitively', seem even less desirable than reaching tentative conclusions with imperfect analytical tools. At least the latter course is likely to lead to further understanding of the problem, even if not to a solution, so long as all those concerned with policy remain aware of the limitations of the argument. It was with this in mind that two *ad hoc* approaches to the second-best problem were developed, one based on maximising market surplus, and the other on Ralph Turvey's method of correcting for discrepancies in associated industries. Both of these are welcome in providing some positive guidance, though both are limited in their application and in the area of Government policy which they cover.

Piecemeal approaches are also needed in determining what rate of discount should be used to extend efficiency conditions to a dynamic situation in which the distribution of resources through time, as well as within the community at any one moment, is important. The problem arises from Government policy and imperfect money markets which result in several candidates for the most appropriate discount rate. As in most second-best problems there is no one obvious solution, though a general compromise can be attempted. One important principle is to recognise that there may not in any case be a unique best rate for all purposes and that different rates can be appropriate in different circumstances.

The only sensible course for an economist to take after considering the immense problems involved in analysing welfare seems to be cautious progress towards some positive conclusion, with consciousness of the limitations and assumptions involved; where possible the results should be tested for sensitivity to changes in these various assumptions. Indeed there are likely to be a number of factors in the problem about which the economist is uncertain, and the argument has so far made no allowance for these, since projects have been assumed riskless (apart from a brief mention of the problems of forecasting inflation). The theory of risk is an extensive area, and there are various techniques by which allowance for risk can be incorporated in Paretian theory; however, these are generally less useful in public policy decisions than more *ad hoc* approaches, so the subject is included in the next chapter and treated primarily in practical terms. These techniques extend the theory of first- and second-best welfare criteria presented in the first four chapters rather than fundamentally altering it. Perhaps this basic theory outlined above can best be appreciated by summarising the difficulties in three stages:

(*a*) concentration on efficiency criteria to the total exclusion of others is bound to result in an unbalanced conclusion;

(*b*) even efficiency criteria are unlikely to be straightforward, theoretically or practically, in the second-best situation faced by practical policy-makers; and

(*c*) no obvious reconciliation of these issues is available.

In the past both economists and politicians have been tempted to consider only one side of the problem, either exaggerating or dismissing the difficulties, and suggesting an unbalanced conclusion, or none at all. One way in which these inconclusive theoretical arguments can be used to guide policy decisions, and how Governments have tackled the problem since the war, form the basis of the next four chapters in Part Two.

Part Two

Policy

Chapter 6

Investment Policy

The previous five chapters have discussed how principles based on economic theory can be developed to act as guidelines for public policy decision-making. The various arguments showed clearly some problems of applying 'abstract' economic ideas to the practical world, even though there was no detailed attempt to develop policy rules as such. That is the objective of this and the next three chapters, and many more difficulties will arise in the move towards interpreting as concrete policy criteria the principles developed earlier. The division of decision-making areas between the four chapters of this section is largely for convenience, since it is impossible to consider any part of public policy in isolation from the rest, but without some categorisation the problem becomes very unwieldy.

One major type of decision to be made in the public sector is how many resources to invest in which projects. The basic problem is similar to that faced in private industry, namely how far present consumption should be sacrificed for future returns and where such sacrifice can most effectively be used.

Because of the similarity of the decisions some of the criteria for investment assessment are the same in both sectors of industry, and so part of the general theory of investment is relevant to the public sector; but there are also important differences between private and public investment, so that some criteria used in private firms are not suitable for application in Government and nationalised-industry projects. Therefore the discussion in this chapter of the best criteria for public-sector investment omits many ideas which are appropriate in the private sector but not elsewhere, though the techniques outlined here can be applied to any industry.

The differences between the two types of investment decision are a result of the different possibilities and constraints faced by each sector. Some arise merely from the fact that private firms operate within a competitive market where they must struggle for funds and for survival, while public industries are shielded from such direct competition (even though the Government may impose its own controls). Thus a private firm may find its funds are limited to a level below those it could otherwise profitably invest because money is either not available in sufficient quantities (through imperfect markets) or it can only be borrowed at prohibitively high costs in terms of rate of interest or public confidence. There may also be periods in which a private firm is unwilling to undertake any investment because the economic future looks bleak, and any unnecessary outgoings are avoided to ensure survival. (It has been one of the Government's greatest problems in the early 1970s to stimulate investment in such a pessimistic atmosphere.) Meanwhile Government expenditure is unlikely to be quite so drastically affected in the same way; for although budgets may be cut and economic objectives tightened, the consequences of failing to achieve targets is not so immediate for the concern itself as is bankruptcy in the private sector. The adverse effects of such failure are most likely to be macroeconomic (perhaps adding to inflation or taxes) rather than directly crippling to the firm or sector concerned. Indeed in some cases financial losses may mean a transfer of benefits within the economy (perhaps from taxpayer to consumer) rather than being surrendered altogether as it appears private losses are. (This is one reason, discussed in greater detail later in the chapter, sometimes used for recommending a rate of discount in the public sector lower than that suggested by market forces.) Because of greater access to funds and less drastic implications of losses, investment decisions in the public sector are usually more flexible than in the private sector.

However, public-sector investment appraisal often involves its own unique difficulties. One of these stems from the very characteristics involved in operating on different commercial principles from those of private enterprise. This means that while private firms can usually estimate receipts from an investment by calculating the value of resulting sales, in the public sector it may be necessary for adjustments to be made before receipts truly reflect benefit to society; indeed in some instances (for example health, education and defence) most of the 'product' is not sold on the market, so that entirely different criteria are needed to evaluate its worth. Even in industries in which the output *is* sold to consumers, non-optimal pricing policies may render necessary some recalculation of value; similar problems arise if social costs are not fully reflected by private costs to the industry (one technique to allow for such circumstances is discussed in Chapter 8). This illustrates the interdependence of investment and pricing criteria which is not always clearly understood. It exists in both private and public industry, but classical theory treats its realisation as 'automatic' in private enterprise. Here the profit-maximising entrepreneur sets marginal cost equal to marginal revenue, and at the same time invests resources so long as the present value of returns exceeds costs; these two policies ensure that he maximises profits at any point in time and in relating future and present net benefits. He cannot, of course, determine what net receipts will be until he has estimated the quantity sold and the price he can expect in each time period; these he must calculate from estimated costs and demand – both of which depend on the amount he offers on the market. Thus in private firms there exists an intimate link between pricing and investment decisions, though it is seldom made explicit; the assumptions of classical economic theory ensure that the interdependence exists and that internal consistency is achieved in the solution.

In the public sector, however, no such 'automatic' procedure operates, and in deciding investment and pricing criteria it is important to ensure consistency. The mutual interdependence of these policies is not always recognised by politicians and economists, some of whom discuss the problem as if it were two separate issues. From the viewpoint of investment the total costs and benefits to society must be estimated, including those which may not be reflected in financial returns (for example if the Government uses a nationalised industry to subsidise a particular sector of society, or there is unavoidable pollution whose cost is not borne by consumers). If the product is sold to consumers part of the benefit can be estimated by the financial return from revenue (assuming that this reflects adequately the worth to consumers), but receipts depend on the quantity sold and the price charged. If, for example, average cost is below marginal cost, prices related to average cost will yield greater sales at lower unit revenue than will marginal-cost pricing; thus, in general, the total revenue will be different in each case (larger or smaller according to whether price elasticity of demand exceeds or is less than unity in the relevant range). But pricing policy also affects investment decisions because price determines the quantity demanded, and except in the unusual case of constant marginal costs this in turn determines the level of costs. So even after deciding on a pricing policy and invest-ment criteria the resulting economic model must be examined with various sets of figures to ensure internal consistency. For example, if marginal-cost pricing is chosen as a policy, and investment proceeds so long as it yields net benefits, demand must first be estimated at each point in the future; the cost of meeting it determines marginal cost, which in turn will become the price faced by consumers; assuming that price elasticity of demand exceeds zero, this may change the original assumption for demand and so require the calculations to be altered. Only when all the variables agree with each other will the in-ternal consistency of the profit-maximising private entrepreneur be achieved.

Even more basic an inconsistency, with serious consequences for planning in the industry concerned, may arise if investment is carried out assuming one pricing policy, and a different criterion is used to price the product on the market. In the previous example, where average cost was less than marginal cost, consider a situation in which investment in the industry was made on a marginal-cost-pricing assumption, but prices were set below this, at average cost. If the original investment decisions were internally consistent, provision for output will be less than the demand stimulated by a lower price, so some demand will not be met by available capacity; this means either that rationing or expensive short-term measures to increase output are necessary if price is to be kept at average cost, and this latter course will continue until the average cost, and hence the price, rise to a level at which demand equals output. Clearly this type of inconsistent plan-ning almost inevitably leads to bottlenecks of supply and expensive production techniques, and does not reflect the best use of resources. (No attempt is made here to compare the merits of the two pricing rules suggested; these are discussed in other chapters.) The moral for the economist is to ensure that the models of investment and pricing are both theoretically and practically consistent with each other; too often these have been treated as separate and distinct issues with un-fortunate results.

One common characteristic of public-sector investment has been suggested in the previous paragraph. It tends to involve large discrete units of equipment which limits flexibility in changing output in the short term. Consideration of the nature of nuclear electricity production, the provision of hospitals and road-building illustrates this facet of public-sector output well. Thus public-sector projects frequently involve careful planning and the commitment of large amounts of resources to specialised uses, with the particular problems of risk (considered in greater detail later in the chapter) which this entails. It may help to clarify the issues if we first consider how best to assess riskless private projects. This is closely related to the discussions of Chapter 4, since of course the main issue of investment decisions hinges on the relationship of costs and benefits at different times.

One way of assessing the value of investment, sometimes used in private industry, is to calculate a rate of profitability (for example profit as a percentage of investment costs); this helps to ensure the most profitable use of funds where these are limited as in much private investment, but is less suitable for public-sector projects where such constraints do not apply. In such cases of little effective limit to funds, there are two obvious candidates for assessing projects, each of which has been advocated for use in public industries and Government departments.

The first involves the estimation of the net present value (N.P.V.) of each project (the detailed procedure is illustrated in an example in the appendix to this chapter). The costs and benefits in each time period are forecast, the net benefit for each year converted to present value by the use of an appropriate discount rate, and the worth of the project calculated by subtracting present-value costs from benefits. Since all costs and benefits have been included in the estimation, this figure represents the over-all gain from the investment in present-value terms (including, at least in principle, non-financial rewards and penalties). Theoretically any project yielding a positive present-value net benefit should then be undertaken since society will receive a net gain from it. The approach outlined above is straightforward enough in theory, but its execution raises a number of awkward questions. One of the most basic is simply how to value costs and benefits in each time period, even without uncertainty. As we have already seen, public-sector projects often involve the estimation of non-monetary effects, particularly benefits which for the private firm are simply represented by revenue. How, for example, can the worth of a new road or school be easily included, or the benefit of investment bringing employment to an economically depressed area? Similar problems may arise on the cost side since the nature of public projects often involves displacing homes, adversely affecting a local environment or hastening the depletion of the community's resources. This is the type of estimation problem with which cost–benefit analysis is concerned, and Chapters 8, 11, 12 and 13 show how some of these difficulties can be approached. Immense practical problems arise in this area, but attempts to tackle them have improved theory and knowledge, particularly in the last twenty years. Let us then leave more detailed considerations of such issues for later chapters and assume for the time being that costs and benefits have been satisfactorily estimated for each year, even though this is unlikely to be a straightforward procedure.

The next stage is to discount these costs and benefits back to present value, and here both theoretical and practical problems arise in determining the optimum discount rate for each year. In principle there is no reason why this should be identical for each time period, but in practice one discount rate is usually used for the entire life of a project. (An exception to this arises in the 'cut-off' approach to risk discussed below which applies an infinite discount rate to years after the cut-off horizon.) The optimal rate to apply in investment appraisals is fraught with problems, some of which have been discussed in Chapter 4. However even when some principle for discounting is established, arriving at a figure to use in practice may still present difficulties. Table 1 gives some examples of interest and yields in real and money terms over the past few years (though ignoring capital gains and losses) and it is clear that the problems of determining the most appropriate past rate to use as a guide to investors' *ex ante* real expectations (that is a market social time preference rate) are not easily solved. Even more difficult to determine is private industry's expected return on a marginal riskless long-term project, which the arguments presented in Chapter 4 suggest should also influence the Government's discount rate. Probably some figure between zero and 10 per cent real return (as very general limits to expected real returns to investors and industry) is appropriate in the current (1976) high inflation which enhances the attractions of any investment which keeps its real value. However, there are two arguments which suggest that real return to consumers is an inadequate guide to the value of the social time preference rate. One maintains that because individuals are mortal they have a higher discount rate than does society as a whole; this is partially linked with the idea of increased riskiness for an individual's returns than for the benefit to all society, so that individual investors appear 'short-sighted' in their decisions, indicating that the social time preference rate may in practice be lower than that suggested by the market. Conversely it has been argued that the market over-estimates the S.T.P.R. because society can expect to have a gradually increasing standard of living. With a decreasing marginal utility of income this would therefore value relatively less benefits and costs occurring in the future when national product is expected to be higher. To some extent this might be reflected in the market rate since individual investors will also experience the higher standards, though again 'myopia' and the problems of forecasting may lead them to under-estimate this factor; if they do, this suggests that marginal market returns to investors exceed that which represents a marginal

TABLE 1

	Financial Times index of ordinary shares price index	*F.T.* index of ordinary shares earnings yield (per cent)	Rate of increase in Retail Price Index (per cent)	Real earnings (that is allowing for inflation) (per cent)	Bank rate/ minimum lending rate at end year (per cent)
1955	195·0	12·85	5·3	7·1	4½
1956	180·6	15·92	3·7	11·8	5½
1957	188·3	15·04	3·0	11·7	7
1958	181·9	14·96	0·6	14·3	4
1959	250·2	10·82	1·0	9·7	4
1960	318·6	9·02	3·4	5·4	5
1961	319·8	9·62	4·4	5·0	5
1962	285·5	8·88	2·0	6·7	4½
1963	316·9	6·73	3·3	3·3	4
1964	346·9	7·36	4·8	2·4	7
1965	337·3	9·12	3·9	5·0	6
1966	331·9	8·52	2·5	6·9	7
1967	355·0	6·69	4·5	2·1	8
1968	463·3	4·99	5·4	−0·4	7
1969	419·8	5·82	6·4	−0·5	8
1970	361·0	6·54	9·4	−2·6	7
1971	386·2	6·21	5·6	0·6	5
1972	503·8	4·98	7·7	−2·5	9
1973	435·6	*	10·3	*	13
1974	251·2	21·47	18·2	2·8	11½

* Change in definition of yield resulted in no figure for 1973.
SOURCE: *Financial Statistics* (London: H.M.S.O., 1975).

return to society (the S.T.P.R.). In any case a single appropriate return to investors is difficult to ascertain, and, as the principles discussed in Chapter 4 suggest, private opportunity costs should also be taken into account in discounting public investment. In practice, as we shall see in Chapter 9, the Government has recommended real returns of 8 and 10 per cent, though these may be intended more as a reflection of opportunity cost of capital in the private sector than as a compromise between that and the S.T.P.R.; in any case Government forecasts of inflation may tend to under-estimate its value (perhaps for political reasons or through the optimism of human nature and politicians) so that an intended real return of 8 per cent may in practice be rather less, particularly if the public sector is subject to price restraint at a time of general inflation.

The problems of choosing a discount rate in calculating net present values has led some economists to suggest that it can be avoided by the use of an alternative investment criterion – the size of the internal rate of return (I.R.R.). This is a method of ranking projects according to what rate of discount (their internal rate of return) discounts costs and benefits to zero net present value. In this case a unique discount rate for all years is applied, so there is no allowance for possible variations over time. Projects can then be ranked from the highest I.R.R. to the lowest, and carried out in that order. Theoretically all projects showing a return greater than the opportunity cost of capital should then be instituted.

The internal-rate-of-return criterion has a theoretical snag since a unique solution of the discount rate bringing costs and benefits to zero cannot be guaranteed. (An example of one such problem is given in the appendix to this chapter.) However, if there are multiple solutions it is not usually difficult to identify the relevant value, and in many ways this criterion is similar to the N.P.V. system. It involves evaluation of costs and benefits in each time period, with all the associated problems, just as the calculation of net present value does. Indeed, if the same rate of discount is used in calculating N.P.V. and as the cut-off rate of return for investment, the two criteria give identical results; for if the appropriate rate of discount is r in each case, projects with an internal rate of return greater than r will yield positive N.P.V., while those whose I.R.R. is less than r will have negative net present value, discounting at r (see the example in the appendix). The initial illusion that I.R.R. avoids the problem of determining a rate of discount is dispelled as soon as a cut-off rate for projects has to be decided.

However, the I.R.R. involves a slightly different emphasis in deciding the best value for *r*. This is usually regarded as the opportunity cost of capital (in the market for private firms, in private investment for the public sector), so in general this would be higher than the compromise rate suggested earlier for use in N.P.V. This means that more projects which would yield positive N.P.V. using the social time preference rate will be abandoned under I.R.R. than under N.P.V. criteria (some will not be carried out even using the latter, since the suggested discount rate lies above the S.T.P.R. but below the opportunity cost of capital). If the argument that the best rate is a compromise between S.T.P.R. and the opportunity cost of capital, then net-present-value techniques offer the most appropriate way of applying it; however, if the opportunity cost of capital in the private sector is to be used in both cases, the two methods are equivalent anyway. The additional flexibility of the N.P.V. criterion in allowing variable discount rates, and the greater ease in understanding the model's techniques, recommend it as the more appropriate method.

One feature common to public investment which may cause problems with either method of investment appraisal, but particularly using I.R.R., arises when projects are interdependent. Thus, for example, a new airport may be considered in conjunction with extending a motorway; each project by itself may give an I.R.R. lower than the cut-off level, while the combined investment could have a higher return. Ranking projects according to the I.R.R. criterion may lead decision-makers to ignore possibilities of combining projects which would together yield greater benefits than the sum of their parts.

One advantage that has been claimed for the internal-rate-of-return approach is that it can be used to include a consideration of risk simply by increasing the cut-off rate of return for projects to be undertaken. This then requires that the best forecasts of costs and returns have a higher internal rate of return (perhaps 2 per cent greater for moderately risky and 4 per cent for highly risky projects). The principle of including considerations of risk by increasing the rate of return is sometimes recommended to ensure that resources are allocated optimally between risky and non-risky projects. However, it is not altogether suitable for this means, and may have undesirable implications for long-term public-sector investment. This is because an increased discount rate has a relatively greater effect in reducing the present value of far-distant costs and benefits than those in the nearer future. In some ways this seems appropriate because there is likely to be greater uncertainty attached to such returns; but it has the effect of penalising projects with long-term benefits stretching far into the future because they become discounted more heavily than benefits arising sooner. A simple example illustrates this fact. Suppose the discount rate is raised from 8 to 10 per cent to allow for some uncertainty in estimating costs and benefits: before the rate is raised the discount rate for ten years time $(1 + 0.08)^{-10}$, is 0.46, and, at the new rate of 10 per cent, becomes $(1 + 0.10)^{-10}$, or 0.39; the addition of 2 per cent to the discount rate thus has the effect of reducing the present value of returns ten years distant by 0.39/0.46, or 0.84. Similarly the discount for costs and benefits in twenty years is changed from 0.21 to 0.15, so the ratio is 0.71, the square of that for half the number of years. Thus, as the years for which returns are estimated receeds into the future, the effect of increasing the discount rate to allow for risk is to reduce the present value more and more. This may have a distorting effect that is best avoided in assessing public-sector projects which typically do involve long-term benefits. Even though it is probably especially difficult to estimate accurately what these will be, to systematically devalue them in present terms may not be the best approach; in particular it is worth considering that if central estimates are made of the costs and benefits, a risky project may involve a chance of surpluses over these forecasts, as well as the possibility of losses. To successively 'scale down' the central estimates as these become more distant does not therefore seem an obvious solution to this uncertainty, at any rate in the public sector. Various techniques allowing for the fact that no project involves costs and benefits which can be forecast perfectly in real terms exist, some more suitable than others for the particular characteristics of public investment.

The fact that nationalised industries and Government departments are not necessarily concerned with avoiding losses (though artificial constraints may be imposed to reflect Government policy) means that risk assessment, as well as more general investment criteria, are more flexible in the public than in the private sector. Some of the problems of comparability with the private sector which have already been discussed for the rate of discount are relevant also in the consideration of risk. In particular the relative riskiness of a project to individuals may be greater than to the community, for while the failure of an investment can involve forfeit of funds to a private investor they may still bring some return to the community at large. This 'pooling' of risk for society suggests that a smaller allowance for possible loss should be made for public projects than for private. This is reinforced by the effect of tax which has already been considered in this chapter and in Chapter 4 in its distorting effect between the public and private sectors. Clearly, in requiring an additional net return to allow for the risk involved in a particular project, a private firm would demand a gross return before tax even above this. Thus much investment with a gross return, which, on average, benefits society as a whole, may not be profitable to private firms and hence be discarded. This raises an issue similar to that discussed in relation to riskless investment where a distortion is bound to occur in using either the private opportunity cost or the S.T.P.R. for discounting. If lower-risk criteria are used in the public sector, because over all it seems such projects will bring net benefits to the community, resources may be diverted away from the private sector where higher returns are available but not carried out because of greater risk aversion and tax liability. The ideal solution would be to stimulate investment in both sectors in such a situation — perhaps by providing some form of insurance for firms undertaking certain kinds of risky investment, or by changing the tax liability. However, equity considerations would suggest that those who make large profits from risky projects should not be treated preferentially with respect to tax, but that those who did badly in such speculative ventures might be given favourable treatment. In the public sector it will probably be difficult to generalise about appropriate risk criteria, for while, mostly, risk aversion may be less than in the private sector, some risks, particularly where they involve severe economic or social consequences for a significant sector of the country (for example a nationalised industry or geographical region), are likely to be avoided by Government. Any generalised 'rule-of-thumb' approach to risky projects seems bound to be inadequate in these circumstances.

One treatment which takes a more general line and is popular with some theorists in this field is the expected-value approach. Using this method a range of returns for each time period and the probability attached to each possible outcome are estimated. Multiplying the quantities by the probability of their occurrence yields expected costs or benefits, and these expected values can be added and discounted to N.P.V. just as for certain returns. The result is then the expected net present value, and, providing the estimates are correct, this represents the average return which would arise in a large number of repetitions of the project; this makes the technique particularly suitable for replacement policy where similar issues arise repeatedly. However, most public-sector decisions are not of this nature, but involve a heavy once-and-for-all commitment of resources. One major problem of using expected values in a 'one-off' long-term project is that the probabilities themselves are extremely difficult to estimate. Apart from the uncertainties involved in a unique project, returns often depend on the state of the economy and technology decades into the future so that forecasting the various outcomes, let alone their exact probabilities, is likely to be fraught with problems. It is unlikely, too, that the Government will attach the same significance to outcomes with similar expected values. For example, a project may involve a small probability of severe social and economic hardship for a sector of the economy, while its greater likelihood of a substantial profit yields a present value similar to that of a project with a high probability of moderate gain; in such a case the Government is likely to prefer the latter project since it does not risk severely adverse results, even though the expected net present values may be identical. In theory, allowance could be made in estimating expected values for aversion to risk of large losses and the forecasts in each case weighted accordingly. In practice it would be difficult to quantify reliably how much the Government wished to avoid particular outcomes (though continued cost–benefit analyses do build up some body of acceptable figures along these lines), and although the resulting single expected value might appear helpful in comparing projects, it is likely to conceal rather than reveal the essential differences between them. Thus the expected-value approach to risk, though useful in the context of repeated similar investments, is not particularly helpful in assessing most public projects.

Another theoretically attractive approach is to use a 'games-theory' model in which the objectives of Government and investors can be used to develop a 'utility index' of various outcomes. However, in practice these are virtually impossible to interpret usefully and so this branch of investment theory is unlikely to be useful. Some details of the theory of the games approach are given by Baumol [1972].

One rather defeatist approach to the particular kinds of uncertainty faced by long-term Government projects is to impose a 'horizon' beyond which costs and benefits are ignored (this is usually about twenty or thirty years in the future). In many ways this is a tempting course, for we have already observed that changes in demand and technology make it very difficult to forecast such distant events, and that increasing the rate of discount to allow for risk decreases their relative importance in the investment calculation. Nevertheless it seems that, however difficult to forecast distant values may be, the assumption that the project ceases to exist at all after a couple of decades (in effect applying an infinite discount rate after this time) is most extraordinary. However imperfect the forecasting, it must be possible to make more realistic estimates than these. There is a particular danger, too, in ignoring distant effects of an investment, especially for long-term projects which are just those for which the horizon cut-off is most likely to be used. There is an increasing tendency amongst economists and engineers, probably reflecting general public opinion, that it is precisely the long-term consequences of investment decisions which should be given more emphasis in assessments rather than ignored. For example, in the problem of exploiting and pricing North Sea gas (which is mentioned in Chapter 10), a solution which ignored the consequences at a time when gas (and later oil) reserves were being exhausted would not only yield misleading solutions now but might leave the country and economy unprepared for the consequences of depletion. Whatever the problems of forecasting the relevant values, to ignore them entirely is both inaccurate and dangerous.

No formal risk criterion seems completely satisfactory for assessing public investment, but one more 'intuitive' approach, while less theoretically appealing, may yield more useful guidelines for assessing and following the development of a project. This is known as a 'sensitivity analysis', and usually starts with 'central' or 'most probable' forecasts of the variables concerned, giving a 'central' solution. However, the study is continued by examining the consequences for the project of changes in key variables — for example prices of competing products, the general state of the economy, the birth rate, the rate of change of technology. Opinions as to changes in each of these factors can then be sought from experts in appropriate fields, so that a range of solutions and outcomes will eventually become apparent. These will usually be analysed and presented by a computer for any project that is at all involved, as most public-sector investments are. The decision-maker is then faced with a number of possible consequences for each project, and while this will give him no simple criterion by which to compare them, it should enable him to have a better understanding of what each entails. It also eliminates the necessity for using a single central forecast or ascribing exact probabilities to various events; to do either will be difficult because of the problems of achieving a consensus, even (or perhaps especially) among 'experts'.

This method has an additional significant advantage in public-investment projects of providing a ready-made monitoring scheme once the project is under way. In practice such monitoring is an important and valuable part of investment management, and if changes in key variables have already been examined their consequences are more readily understood. When the original assessment of the project has been modelled on a computer, even values of variables outside those originally envisaged can be readily tested. A good example of how a sensitivity analysis might have helped in assessing the consequences of changes in public investment arose in the sudden increase in world oil prices at the end of 1973. Such increases had been forecast, but were not expected in most circles until much later and the change had significant consequences throughout industry. However, in a project originally examined through a sensitivity analysis some variation in the timing and amount of oil price increases could have been considered; even if the realised prices had not been exactly forecast and examined, they could easily and quickly be inserted in the model so their implications could be assessed and acted upon. This 'follow-up' facility is not readily available with other investment risk criteria.

Of course the sensitivity analysis by itself does not provide an easy formula for deciding between risky projects with high expected values and safer projects with lower expectations, and it must be used in conjunction with a conventional investment criterion such as maximising net present value. But it allows the decision-maker to bring an intuitive approach to facts and priorities which are often difficult or impossible to quantify reasonably. It also allows the link between the economist and politician to develop more easily than with more formal criteria by enabling them to discuss the issues together; this is often difficult if the economist conducts the factual analysis and then 'hands over' to a politician who must ascribe values to particular events but does not clearly understand the model he is presented. This relationship between economist and politician is one which bedevils much of public-sector practice, and is subject to frequent misunderstandings. It is a problem which raises its head repeatedly in the practice of Government policy, as we shall see throughout the rest of the book. The economist usually recognises that only the politician is competent to make certain judgements on relative values, but may find it frustrating and difficult to incorporate these in his analysis if the politician expresses them in language which lends itself only to qualitative interpretation. The next two chapters, particularly, show how different approaches to the same problem can result in apparently contradictory solutions, and how delicate is the balance between the different criteria which determine Government policy.

Appendix to Chapter 6: Example of Net-Present-Value and Internal-Rate-of-Return Calculation

Many students will have met these investment-appraisal techniques in other contexts, but, for those who have not, a simple example to illustrate the basic method is given below. Consider a project which has an initial cost of £600, with receipts of £200 per annum in the first two years, and £650 in the third year; variable costs amount to £100 per annum, and there is scrap value of £50 when the project ends after three years. This investment is to be assessed to determine whether or not it should be undertaken.

A. Calculation of Net Present Value

Some assumption must be made about the timing of income and expenditure in each time period, and for ease of exposition suppose that these all occur at the end of each year. Then, to consider the present value of the project, it is necessary to bring all quantities to present-value terms by discounting by the appropriate factor. This can be deduced from the following argument.

Assuming all factors can be predicted with certainty in real terms and a 10 per cent per annum rate of interest prevails, £100 now is equivalent to £110 in a year's time, since it could be invested for a return of that amount (in capital and interest) after one year. Similarly this could be re-invested to yield £110 + $\frac{1}{10}$ × £110 after a further year, and so on. Conversely, £100 in two years' time is worth now only that sum of money which, after investment for two years at 10 per cent compound interest, would yield £100. This amount, £X, can be found from the equation

$$X(1 + 0 \cdot 1)^2 = 100,$$

that is

$$X = \frac{100}{(1 + 0 \cdot 1)^2} = 0 \cdot 83.$$

More generally the present value of any sum, S, accruing in n years' time, discounted at rate r, is given by

$$\frac{S}{(1 + r)^n}.$$

We can use this formula to reduce all net benefits from the project outlined above to present value (that is beginning of year 1) terms. Consider first a discount rate of 10 per cent per annum, and the table of costs and benefits (Table 2) derived from the description of the project outlined in the introduction to the appendix.

TABLE 2

Net present value calculated at 10 per cent discount rate (all figures in £)

1	2	3	4	5	6
			Net receipts (column 2 − column 3)	Discount factor	Net present value (column 4 × column 5)
Year	Receipts	Costs			
1	200	600 + 100	−500	$\dfrac{1}{(1 + 0 \cdot 1)} = 0 \cdot 91$	−455
2	200	100	100	$\dfrac{1}{(1 + 0 \cdot 1)^2} = 0 \cdot 83$	83
3	650 + 50	100	600	$\dfrac{1}{(1 + 0 \cdot 1)^3} = 0 \cdot 75$	450
TOTAL NET PRESENT VALUE:					78

The positive figure (£78) for net present value shows that benefits of this scheme outweigh the costs at this discount rate. However, at a 25 per cent discount rate a rather different picture emerges, as Table 3 shows (the first four columns are the same as in Table 2). When discounted at 25 per cent, the present value of costs exceeds present-value benefits, so the project yields negative net benefits, and would not be undertaken on the basis of this assessment. This highlights the importance of using an appropriate rate of discount.

The principles used in Tables 2 and 3 can be extended to any number of time periods, theoretically with different discount rates for each, though in practice a uniform rate is usually employed as in the examples given. By this technique the expected streams of costs and benefits for any project can be translated to the investment's net present value.

TABLE 3

Net present value at 25 per cent discount rate (all figures in £)

1	2	3	4	5	6
Year	Receipts	Costs	Net receipts (column 2 — column 3)	Discount factor	Net present value (column 4 × column 5)
1	200	600 + 100	−500	$\dfrac{1}{(1 + 0 \cdot 25)} = 0 \cdot 80$	−400
2	200	100	100	$\dfrac{1}{(1 + 0 \cdot 25)^2} = 0 \cdot 64$	64
3	650 + 50	100	600	$\dfrac{1}{(1 + 0 \cdot 25)^3} = 0 \cdot 51$	306
TOTAL NET PRESENT VALUE:					− 30

B. Calculation of Internal Rate of Return

In Section *A* specific rates of discount were applied to the expected receipts and costs of a project to yield an estimate of net present value. An alternative approach is to find what rate of discount, when applied, reduces this net present value to zero. This figure is known as the 'internal rate of return', and can be estimated by forming an equation whose roots give appropriate values. Suppose this internal rate of return is r, then discounting the net receipts (shown in column 4 of Tables 2 and 3 above) by $1+r$, raised to the appropriate power, we can form the following equation:

$$\frac{-500}{(1 + r)} + \frac{100}{(1 + r)^2} + \frac{600}{(1 + r)^3} = 0,$$

which becomes $\quad 5(1 + r)^2 - (1 + r) - 6 = 0.$

Solving for r we have $\quad 5r^2 + 9r - 2 = 0$

$$(5r - 1)(r + 2) = 0$$

$$r = +0 \cdot 2$$

or $\quad\quad\quad\quad\quad\quad\quad r = -2.$

Although the equation yields two mathematical roots without any indication which is to be preferred, it is not sensible in economic terms to consider a discount rate of minus 200 per cent, since this is unlikely to correspond with society's observed preferences. Thus in this case the internal rate of return of the project outlined at the beginning of this appendix is 20 per cent. The examples given in Section *A* show that if the project is discounted at a rate lower than this (10 per cent), it yields positive net present value, but if a higher rate is used (25 per cent), the net benefits become negative. Of course by definition any project discounted by its internal rate of return (in this case 20 per cent) will yield zero net present value.

As for the N.P.V. technique the internal-rate-of-return approach can be extended to any number of time periods, though it is difficult to allow for variations in the rate of discount. (Theoretically this would be possible if the relation of discount rates relevant to different time periods was known, for example if it was thought that the rate of return should double after ten years. However, the solution to the equation thus formed would not yield the internal rate of return as it has been defined above, that is a single rate which reduces net present value to zero, and it is difficult to imagine circumstances where a variable rate would be appropriate.) As more time periods are included the equation whose roots yield the internal rate of return becomes more complicated, for example in ten time periods the highest power of r will be nine, and there will generally be nine roots, of which only one is usually appropriate. Thus the theoretical ambiguities increase with the number of time periods, but it is generally obvious which root is applicable, as in the example given above.

The two techniques outlined in this appendix can be seen to be equivalent in many respects; some discussion of their relative merits is contained in the main text of Chapter 6.

Suggestions for Further Reading

K. J. ARROW, 'Discounting and Public Investment Criteria', in *Water Resources Research*, ed. A. V. Kneese and S. C. Smith (Baltimore: Johns Hopkins Press, 1966).

W. J. BAUMOL, 'On the Discount Rate for Public Projects', in *Public Expenditures and Policy Analysis,* ed. R. H. Haveman and J. Margolis (Chicago: Markham, 1970).

W. J. BAUMOL, *Economic Theory and Operations Analysis,* 3rd edn (Englewood Cliffs, N.J.: Prentice-Hall, 1972).

G. CORTI, 'Risk, Uncertainty and Cost Benefit: Some Notes on Practical Difficulties for Project Appraisals', in *Cost Benefit and Cost Effectiveness*, ed. J. N. Wolfe (London: Allen & Unwin, 1973).

M. S. FELDSTEIN, 'Net Social Benefits and the Public Investment Decision', *Oxford Economic Papers*, vol. 16 (1964).

M. S. FELDSTEIN AND J. M. FLEMING, 'The Problem of Time-Stream Evaluation: Present Value versus Internal Rate of Return Rules, *Bulletin of the Oxford University Institute of Economics and Statistics*, vol. 26 (1964).

F. H. KNIGHT, *Risk, Uncertainty and Profit* (New York: Harper & Row, 1921).

S. A. MARGLIN, 'The Social Rate of Discount and the Optimum Rate of Investment', *Quarterly Journal of Economics*, vol. 77 (1963).

A. J. MERRET AND A. SYKES, *The Finance and Analysis of Capital Projects* (London: Longmans, 1963).

E. J. MISHAN, *Elements of Cost Benefit Analysis* (London: Allen & Unwin, 1972).

RALPH TURVEY, 'Present Value vs. Internal Rate of Return', *Economic Journal*, vol. 57 (1963).

Chapter 7

Pricing Policy

The discussion in the previous chapter has already shown that pricing and investment criteria can only sensibly be determined as part of the same policy; they are analysed in separate chapters mainly for convenience and because traditionally they have been considered as different issues, despite the relationship which we have already traced. For revenue depends on the price which is charged, and so without a pricing policy an enterprise cannot estimate income. Similarly a firm wishing to follow a particular pricing policy, say marginal-cost pricing, needs to know the level of the relevant costs. These depend on the pattern of production determined by investment, while the optimum investment pattern itself depends on anticipated demand; however, demand is determined by the price charged, so the problem is a reiterative one in which the whole line of argument must be repeated until the pricing, investment and demand variables are mutually compatible.

In particular it is clear that one of the main decision variables discussed in both Chapters 4 and 6, the rate of discount to be used in assessing investment projects, also has a central role in determining optimal prices. For these must be related to costs (usually average or marginal costs) in some way, and the evaluation of resources used in the investment depends on how costs and benefits are related at different times. This can best be illustrated from the case of North Sea fuel depletion, discussed at greater length in Chapter 10, for with a limited natural resource its use at one point of time evidently incurs the opportunity cost of being unable to consume it at a later date. The value of this opportunity cost in present-value terms depends chiefly (though not solely) on the discount rate applied, so that any cost-related price would also be affected by the rate of discount. This relationship between price and discount rate is true of all investment projects, though it is not always so obvious. It is clear, then, that because of the interrelated nature of cost and investment criteria these cannot sensibly be separated in practice, even though for ease of exposition the decision-making is here examined in turn from each of these two aspects.

There are some instances of public policy where pricing criteria are not directly relevant to decision-making – most obviously when the output of the industry is not sold in a market situation, as in the health and education sectors. In these cases some other criterion apart from revenue must be used to determine the value of a project. A similar problem may arise if the product or service is not entirely free but is subsidised by Government so that revenue does not reflect its full value to society. Some of the special problems associated with such projects are discussed in the next chapter on cost–benefit analysis. There remain, however, several industries in the public sector whose main function is to sell their products in a market context. It is for these (fuel, transport, and so on) that some pricing policy needs to be specified.

Proposals for public-sector pricing have usually come in one of three forms: average-cost pricing which ensures that industries cover their costs; marginal-cost pricing on 'efficiency' grounds; and some form of price discrimination between consumers as a compromise between the other two policies. Some general welfare arguments have been considered in the first part of the book, and the way in which these various policies have been incorporated in Government attitudes is discussed further in Chapter 9. Clearly the arguments presented here are part of the broader discussion throughout the book.

Some theoretical arguments in favour of marginal-cost pricing have already been presented in Chapter 3. Their basis is normally that such a policy will maximise efficiency – either for the country as a whole, or for a particular industry or group of industries. However, the General Theory of the Second Best suggests that in practice marginal-cost pricing is unlikely to optimise the distribution of resources since imperfections in the economy would indicate a departure from marginal-cost pricing even in those industries where it is still attainable. Thus the 'over-all efficiency' argument is rather weak in practice, though there is no guidance as to what policy would achieve the second best. Even within one sector there are probably sufficient distortions from Paretian-optimal conditions to involve the second-best argument. We are therefore left with three reasonable justifications for using marginal-cost pricing: distortions may be so small and our alternative policy so uncertain that we can proceed as if in a first-best position; if eventually a first-best position may be established throughout the economy, marginal-cost prices in some sectors would be a move in the right direction; and marginal-cost pricing at least maximises market surplus for the consumers and producers of the industry concerned.

A significant argument against marginal-cost pricing arose in industries where it would result in substantial deficits or surpluses and this gave support to an average-cost-pricing criterion. Analysis presented in Chapter 3 has shown that the market-surplus and efficiency arguments in favour of marginal-cost pricing are valid in such cases, even when average costs exceed marginal costs and a producer loss is incurred. It does, however, involve distributional changes in economic welfare on a fairly arbitrary basis (that is a transfer to consumers of goods produced under decreasing-average-cost conditions and from those who buy 'increasing-cost' products). The extent to which this is a disadvantage of marginal-cost pricing in these cases (one of which is likely to prevail in most industries) depends on how far the Government can easily encompass the redistribution within its wider programme of subsidy and taxation without decreasing efficiency by distorting margins elsewhere in the economy. It remains a popular contention among politicians and businessmen that the existence of losses in such cases not only calls for subsidies from the Exchequer but lowers the morale of management in the industry concerned, thus leading to inefficiency. (This is using the term 'inefficiency' in the 'popular' sense of keeping costs as low as possible, rather than in the more specialised Paretian sense employed previously; the latter use is normally assumed to include the former, as costs are taken to be the minimum that need to be incurred to achieve a given output.) How far do these criticisms of need for subsidy and lowering of morale in practice invalidate the marginal-cost-pricing theory? We have already seen that a loss-making industry needs some funds from general sources in order to continue production. The redistribution issue may be ignored following Pareto's contention that the distribution of welfare is not the concern of an economist investigating the maximisation of efficiency; surely, it can be argued, some other Government department can take the subsidy into account in determining the distribution of wealth. This may indeed be true in practice in the long run, but in the more immediate future subsidising nationalised industries is likely to present more of a problem both politically and economically. Even if we allow only arguments of efficiency as relevant we cannot ignore the fact that subsidies to the public sector, unless coincident exactly with the redistribution of resources within the economy that the Government would want to bring about in any case, mean that taxes must be raised to cover the losses. Economists have spent many years searching for the 'non-marginal tax' which will have no effects on efficiency, but such taxes are extremely rare, and usually rather inequitable — a poll tax is probably the only true example. It would not be feasible to raise all the necessary funds by such means, and so maintaining efficiency in public-sector pricing may be possible only at the expense of distorting margins elsewhere in the economy. Some writers (Fleming [1944] for example) have suggested that losses in decreasing-cost industries could be covered by surplus from those in which marginal cost exceeds average costs; however, the problems of redistribution and extracting the surplus with no marginal effect remain. It is worth emphasising that not all nationalised industries would make a deficit using marginal-cost pricing, though the existence of substantial surpluses might cause as much political embarrassment, for different reasons; in particular industries involved in extracting raw materials (coal, gas and later the British National Oil Corporation) are likely to use better and cheaper reserves first, causing increased costs as production is expanded.

Even where losses are made, the distributional effects of marginal-cost pricing are likely to vary *within* the public sector. The fuel industries, for example, draw their largest domestic consumers from the wealthier members of society, since they are more likely to be able to afford a high standard of heating. Subsidies to such consumers are unlikely to be supporting those whom society would most like to benefit. (It is interesting to note, however, that the converse of this contention, that small users of a particular fuel are likely to be poor, is not necessarily true. Many users of small quantities of gas or electricity use them as a second fuel, for example consumers with gas water and central heating are likely to use less electricity than those who cannot afford space heating but use an immersion heater (or an electric cooker) for water heating. Thus attempts to shield the poor from the effects of price increases by subsidising small consumers may be misguided.) An analogous political issue exists where payment for free hospital beds for all (ignoring any controversy about private patients queue-jumping or receiving subsidies from the National Health Service) is unlikely to discriminate in favour of the rich, and may have the opposite effect if poorer sections of the community are more liable to ill health, and admission is on the basis of need. (Though in practice it seems likely that those with more economic resources may have better access to such facilities through their greater understanding and fluency.) We might in any case view all ill people as 'disadvantaged' members of society to whom we would wish to extend subsidised facilities. Thus the effect of public-sector subsidies on the distribution of welfare will probably be different in various departments, and may often require detailed analysis for full appreciation. For example, in the transport and fuel industries the effect of subsidies must be considered not only in the domestic market but for industrial users too, and the effect on the distribution of welfare in this case will depend on who consumes the products of those industries receiving most subsidy. Obviously there is a practical limit on how far the effects of a subsidy can be pursued, but the repercussions often go considerably beyond the most obvious immediate effects, and it may be necessary to estimate them to achieve a complete understanding of the issues.

The anti-subsidy argument is used most vociferously in the case of loss-making industries, but the converse problem arises if marginal costs exceed average costs and marginal-cost pricing results in a profit in excess of the industry's needs for investment, as has been suggested could happen in some fuel industries. Here the money is distributed to the general taxpayer by relieving pressure on the Treasury, and economic welfare is transferred from the consumers of the product to the general community. This is not likely to cause difficulties for an industry in the fuel sector where the largest contributors to the surplus would probably be 'comfortably off'. But if such a surplus were to arise in another sector, say part of the transport industries known to be used mainly by poor consumers, its redistribution to the general public might cause more difficulties. Indeed considering that one of the philosophical justifications for nationalisation of monopolies is to prevent the 'exploitation' of consumers and high monopoly profits, a large surplus from such an industry, even resulting from marginal-cost pricing rather than profit maximisation, is likely to be politically controversial. However, such profits could be used to offset other tax burdens and thus bring margins closer to Paretian criteria elsewhere in the economy; they may therefore lend themselves more readily to increasing efficiency than do deficits. Nevertheless there are likely to be real practical problems involved in either substantial losses or surpluses in the public sector; and although adjustments can be made to allow for these in the long run, they may pose more immediate problems of organisation. *A priori* this seems to be an argument for careful examination of the likely effect of marginal-cost pricing, rather than for its immediate abandonment.

The disadvantages of setting prices equal to marginal costs where these diverged from average costs was given a slightly different emphasis by Coase [1946], who was worried about how the investment decision could be optimised in cases where the total costs were not covered (or were exceeded) by total revenue. This is a difficult area, and is likely to require Government guidance to ensure that a product is produced if the total community benefits exceed total costs, even if in financial terms the industry bears a loss. Of course such a decision is not always straightforward, as the discussions in Chapters 6 and 8 show. (Coase was also concerned about the redistribution of income and the marginal effects of taxation needed for subsidies, which have been considered above.) Coase's own solution to ensure that price equals marginal cost but that total costs are covered in decreasing-cost industries was to introduce multi-part tariffs, with pre-marginal units more expensive than the marginal purchases whose price would reflect marginal cost. This is an attractive compromise which is discussed at the end of the chapter, but first there are more direct problems of marginal-cost pricing to be considered.

One is that public-sector losses may lower the morale of management and so lead to inefficiency and increased costs. This contention arises from the private-sector criterion that profits are the mark of success, and that losses indicate a failed firm (as they do for private industry). It seems highly probable that if society takes the same attitude to the public sector then workers in an industry whose pricing policy results in a loss, and are thereby judged to be failures, are indeed likely to suffer a lowering of morale. This in turn may lead to a lack of incentive to keep costs down and to look for innovations as the most able employees move out of the industry to more 'rewarding' jobs. However, it seems a waste of the public sector to treat it merely as a group of industries which happen to be in public ownership but otherwise to be judged as private firms; and if it is part of the public-sector policy, and is accepted as such by both management and society, that some industries follow pricing criteria which result in losses, there seems no reason why the industries should become discouraged. This depends partly on the expected losses being clearly defined so that the industry knows what targets it is being set. Indeed there is little evidence that the morale of the railway industry suffered significantly as a result of losses incurred in the 1960s, though it probably was affected by being expected to meet the incompatible targets of subsidising some lines while realising a profit over all. The inevitability, and even desirability, of incurring losses now seems generally accepted by Government, management and workers in British Rail. However, it is difficult to establish just what does affect morale; it seems reasonable to suppose, though, that it is not necessarily adversely affected by losses where these are recognised as an inevitable result of pricing and investment policies, and may even be taken as an indication that public priorities are being realised.

The arguments against marginal-cost pricing have a well-entrenched tradition since the war, and the Government's own somewhat reluctant move towards marginal-cost pricing is discussed in Chapter 9. There seems a pervasive instinct that average-cost pricing is better because it enables the industries to pay their way and avoid subsidies, thus fulfilling one of their statutory obligations. There seems no reason to conform to this view, however, if a more open-minded attitude towards nationalised industries, their purposes and management is pursued.

One recurring red herring in the pricing controversy is whether long-term or short-term costs are to be followed, particularly when marginal-cost pricing is recommended. The classical theoretical derivation of long-run cost curves shows that if previous planning has successfully led to the optimum plant size, long-run average and marginal costs will each be the same as their short-run equivalents. However, in practice there may well be a considerable discrepancy. In this case should short-run or long-run costs be used to determine prices? If average-cost pricing is being used on the basis that it will avoid the occurrence of surplus or loss, and leave the industry 'self-contained', then clearly all costs used for accounting must be included in calculating prices, including fixed costs. Thus it is usually long-run average costs which are relevant, though this may not be the case if, for example, a depreciation period shorter than the economic life of assets has been used and productive equipment has been fully amortised. Accounting costs would then regard the use of such capital as free, while the economist might consider how their use would accelerate the need to replace them. Thus long-run average economic and accounting costs will not always coincide, so even using long-run average-cost pricing does not guarantee a zero accounting balance.

If marginal-cost pricing is to be used, it is generally accepted that it is long-run costs which are relevant. The important costs in this case are, quite simply, those whose incurrence is in question. Thus we should look at all the costs which will be undertaken as a result of supplying the marginal unit. In exceptional cases this may not involve capital expenditure, as in a decreasing-demand industry in which no renovation or replacement of machinery is needed. Such a situation did arise in the town gas industry when the advent of natural gas resulted in the premature obsolescence of town gas plant, so an increase in demand in non-converted areas could easily be met from existing equipment (though the issue was complicated by the fact that accepting additional town gas demand would involve a commitment to supply natural gas at a later date, which would involve capital expenditure). Most marginal supply involves some expenditure on capital equipment, and so the relevant marginal costs usually do include this element; but the usual distinction between 'fixed' and 'variable' costs is not helpful in determining marginal costs, and using the basic principles of how a demand variation affects total system costs is the only reliable way of determining the correct marginal-cost price.

Because of the particular character of some nationalised industries, a discussion associated with this long-run/short-run controversy occupied several of the original advocates of marginal-cost pricing (see, for example, Hotelling [1938]). Many nationalised industries are involved in large and indivisible capital expenditure (for example rails and rolling stock, electricity-generating plant) and also face demand which varies according to the time of day or the season. Thus there are occasions when the capital equipment is not used fully, and so marginal units incur no provision of capital equipment; similarly, even at times of peak demand, because capital expenditure is in large discrete amounts, only at certain critical levels of demand will its provision be in question. For example, once a train is provided it will not be until the first carriage is full that significant further expenditure is needed to carry additional passengers. Thus a pedantic interpretation of marginal-cost pricing might imply that the first passenger at the ticket office should pay for the engine and first carriage to be available for the journey, successive passengers using the first carriage should pay only the cost of wear and tear on seats, etc. and the passenger who necessitated the use of a second carriage should bear the cost of its provision, and so on. Similarly in a new housing estate to be supplied with electricity the first occupant would bear the costs of providing a mains supply to the area, and the rest of the consumers merely the costs of extending the supply to them. Since some forward planning is required it is comparatively rare to find the capacity of a system stretched to its limit so that additional expenditure is required to accommodate new consumers; there is usually at least standing room on a train, and gas and electricity mains often provide sufficient excess capacity to allow for some increase in demand. Indeed it is common to install facilities, which residents will not necessarily choose to use, routinely to all new houses even though some (it is not practicable to discover in advance, which) will not be used. This is cheaper than installing new telephone lines or gas services only when consumers ask for them, but does lead to some ambiguity in defining marginal costs; the most reasonable solution seems to be that of dividing the total costs of capital provision between the number of consumers who take up the option of using the facilities; as explained above this will generally be cheaper than the cost of providing them 'to order'. However, this system of planning means that in practice very few consumers directly cause capital expenditure by their own decisions and so a literal marginal-cost price would vary considerably between consumers. The only sensible interpretation in this case is to consider not individual consumers but an average 'type' of consumer and calculate the additional expenditure incurred by the addition of several such consumers or patterns of demand. Thus it is seen as sensible to attribute the cost of maintaining track and providing trains to all consumers whose demand gives rise to the necessity for running a railway system. Of course the train will run whether a particular individual travels on it or not (for one thing it is time-tabled in advance to do so) but all passengers pay not only for their own individual journey but also for the facilities to be provided to enable that journey to occur whenever they choose. Similarly the costs of bringing gas or electricity to a housing estate should be attributed to all consumers who are likely to demand these services, although as for trains the facilities will be determined before individual patterns of demand are known. The justification for this averaging procedure is partly to facilitate equity as well as the smooth operation of the system. Here is a case where literal application of Paretian criteria is abandoned on pragmatic grounds; but while this seems the only sensible way of approaching the problem it does not satisfy a pedantic interpretation of Paretian efficiency. The difficulty arises from the inappropriateness of the classical definition of efficiency in this case: for, in practice, to install facilities only as they are demanded would require the expenditure of more resources than supplying all potential consumers with services. The main problem here is that of identifying which residents (including the successors of the initial purchasers) will require facilities. In such circumstances the most appropriate definition of efficiency seems to be that system of satisfying demand which incurs the minimum use of resources.

The issue is somewhat different in relating marginal costs to seasonal or daily variations in demand, for here different types of demand can be distinguished, rather than the system consisting of several similar demand patterns in which only the order in which they are satisfied determines the allocation of expenditure. For example, it is possible to identify different patterns of cost from peak train travel, when the system is already used to capacity, and demand for rail journeys at off-peak times. Similarly marginal demand for electricity incurs different costs at peak demand and when there is spare capacity (provided for peak but unused), at night for example. (This difference has been reflected in some white-meter off-peak tariffs in the United Kingdom in recent years.) The argument here about different peak and off-peak costs has become involved in the long-run/short-run cost controversy since the issues are superficially similar. At times of peak demand, supplying an additional unit involves capital expenditure to provide more capacity, whereas if excess capacity is available no such capital expense is necessary. Thus it appears as if it is appropriate to talk about long-run marginal costs at peak, and short-run marginal costs at other times. There are two errors in this approach. The most important is a methodological mistake in using the long-run/short-run concept, based on different constraints in planning production, to a situation at one point in time where it is demand rather than production variations which determine the appropriate rate. The second misconception is a popular assumption that off-peak marginal demand never involves capital expenditure since there is always excess capacity available; although it is true that marginal off-peak demand never *requires* capital expenditure because of the existence of excess capacity in the system, it may cause a change in the optimum mix of equipment and so involve some capital investment. For example, in the electricity industry demand is met by a mixture of capital-expensive cheap-to-run plant for base-load demand, and cheaper-to-provide but more-expensive-to-run equipment for peak demand, these latter being used less intensively than the former. An increase in near-peak demand when base-load equipment is already used to capacity clearly could be met by more intensive use of the equipment with expensive running costs, but the changed demand might make it more sensible to increase the provision of capital-expensive plant used to meet the base load. Thus capital expenditure might well be involved. It is therefore clear that the peak/non-peak split is not equivalent to the long-run/short-run distinction, and that meeting non-peak marginal demand may involve some capital expense.

The existence of peak and non-peak demand patterns in many nationalised industries raises the question of how far a marginal-cost tariff should attempt to discriminate between these different times. Most of the discussion on this aspect has concentrated on the electricity industry, and this is probably where the issues are most clearly seen. Demand for electricity varies both daily and seasonally, and at any one time the marginal costs of production are those of the plant being used to meet marginal demand; similarly transmission costs vary according to how heavily the system is being used, so there is almost continuous variation in the costs of supply. To reflect these in a continuously variable tariff would not only be virtually impracticable and very expensive but would also probably confuse the consumer rather than provide a clear signal about costs. One way to give the consumer an option to reduce his contribution to peak consumption is by making an agreement with him in advance that fuel will be temporarily disconnected at times of heavy demand, in exchange for a cheaper tariff. In Australia such a system has been implemented in the electricity industry by installing special circuits for heating appliances; these can then be disconnected by the suppliers for continuous periods of up to half an hour, subject to a maximum total disconnection in any one period. Thus the consumer contracts in advance to economise on peak purchases but leaves the timing of his reduced consumption to the electricity supplier. Clearly such a scheme would not be feasible for a fuel such as gas which cannot safely be cut off and reconnected, nor for electricity without a separate continuous supply for lighting and power functions; but it is a feasible way of reducing peak consumption in appropriate circumstances, and enables the consumer to choose to reduce his bill (through a cheaper unit price for electricity) in exchange for lower peak consumption.

If such a scheme is not feasible and continuously variable tariffs are too involved to give consumers a clear message, one possibility is to provide a single tariff which shows average marginal costs throughout the day and year, though this would not convey to the consumer that at some times an increase in demand would involve the use of many more resources than at other times when the system is less intensively used. The best solution appears to lie somewhere between the two extremes of single and continuously variable tariffs, and is likely to vary in different industries. The British electricity industry, for example, has followed a policy of reflecting diurnal fluctuations in cost by a day/night tariff, but does not provide seasonal tariffs for domestic consumers. The optimum policy is likely to depend on two factors: the expense of introducing a variable tariff and the extent to which demand is sensitive to price variations. Clearly it would not be sensible to involve more resources in implementing a tariff than could be saved by its influence on demand patterns; if demand is more closely related to average annual costs of consumption than to fluctuations in tariffs at particular times of year, it may not be worth reflecting the finer changes in marginal costs. Considerable discussion has taken place on peak-load pricing, and some of the issues are illustrated in the peak-load-pricing example given in Chapter 11.

Another cost distinction often made in public-sector policy discussions, and examined theoretically in Part One, is the distinction between private and social costs. To determine the appropriate marginal cost, the government may wish to direct an industry to include some costs other than the private costs of production it bears itself. An example of this arises in the use of North Sea gas where, because of the system through which the British Gas Corporation buys gas from the oil companies, its price bears no scarcity premium. On the other hand, because gas is a limited resource, consumers using it now should take into account that they thereby deprive the community of the option of using it in the future. Thus the Gas Corporation should add on to its costs of production an element to allow for this scarcity premium before designing appropriate tariffs for the consumer. How this can be calculated is shown in Chapter 10, and some of the problems of determining marginal social costs where these differ from private costs also arise in Chapter 8 on cost–benefit analysis.

This chapter has centred on the problems involved in determining marginal costs, but the discussion would be incomplete without mentioning one proposed compromise between marginal- and average-cost pricing in cases of decreasing average costs, suggested by Coase [1964] and mentioned earlier in this chapter. This seeks to recover the average costs of production from the users of a particular product so that no subsidy is needed, while charging marginal costs on marginal units. This can be achieved by means of a multi-part tariff which

collects sufficient revenue from consumers on pre-marginal units to recover the difference between average and marginal costs, but charges only marginal costs on later units. The standard charges for gas and electricity are multi-part tariffs of this type (though probably not designed primarily to reflect marginal costs nor to maximise revenue). This system is a practicable compromise if consumers can easily be divided according to demand patterns so each consumer faces a tariff with marginal costs reflected at his level of marginal demand, and if consumers base demand on marginal rather than average costs of consumption. In most cases, however, one of these criteria fails to apply, usually the latter. In electricity consumption, for example, although the marginal tariff element may influence how intensively an appliance is used, the average cost of, say, heating by a particular fuel is likely to be the main factor in determining whether electricity is used for such a purpose. This type of decision (that is whether to use electricity or oil for heating, electricity or gas for cooking, and hence the types of appliance bought) is the main determinant of the quantity of each fuel used, and so a tariff which does not reflect the marginal annual cost of using a particular source of power or heat, as well as the marginal cost of using existing appliances more or less intensively, is likely to constrain consumers' decisions away from the most efficient pattern. Thus, despite their apparent attractions multi-part tariffs are likely to prove difficult to implement, and may not truly reflect those marginal costs which should determine consumption.

The relation between average and marginal costs is clearly an important aspect of pricing policy, and we have already mentioned one factor of relevance which can cause misunderstanding between accountants and economists – the issue of depreciation. This is a technique designed to allocate the cost of capital equipment over its lifetime; it has traditionally consisted of attributing a certain proportion of the historic cost of purchasing assets to each year for a time usually much shorter than their expected physically productive life. As inflation has increased, the shortfall between the stock of funds provided by depreciation and those needed for replacement several years later has been recognised, so replacement cost depreciation (basing the allocation of funds on the cost of buying a new machine at current prices) has become more prevalent, though by no means universal. The economist's concept of the cost of using a machine differs slightly from the accountant's since he would wish to measure in some way the decrease in value of the machine, that is in its second-hand value and/or potential earning power, through its use in a particular period. In practice it is not likely to be feasible to estimate this for each machine, plant and building in each time period, so some more *ad hoc* method of allocating capital costs may be necessary. It should be noted that although provision under such a system is likely to 'keep pace' with inflation, there is no guarantee that the cost of a replacement machine will be exactly covered in conditions of changing technology and imperfect markets. However, an accounting replacement cost depreciation system would probably reflect economic criteria reasonably well.

Depreciation systems have been mentioned because they will clearly affect the calculation of costs and prices, especially in a capital-intensive industry. In particular much of the difference between an accounting average-cost price and that suggested by marginal costs may be due to differences in depreciation techniques; this is especially likely to be the case where much of the capital equipment is old, as in many nationalised industries, and already amortised under traditional historic-cost techniques, while an economist would still attribute some cost to its continued use. The Government's own attitude to this issue can be followed in Chapter 9.

What this chapter has tried to show is that pricing policies in the public sector are unlikely to be clear-cut. Marginal-cost pricing may have some theoretical justification but could often involve accounting losses, redistribution of welfare and substantial problems of interpretation in practice. Some of these, particularly where social and private costs do not coincide, are examined in the next chapter, which re-unites the pricing and investment decisions.

Suggestions for Further Reading

E. W. CLEMENS, 'Price Discrimination in Decreasing Cost Industries', *American Economic Review*, vol. 31 (1941).

R. H. COASE, 'The Marginal Cost Controversy', *Economica*, vol. 13 (1946).

HAROLD HOTELLING, 'The General Welfare in Relation to Problems of Taxation and of Railway and Utility Rates', *Econometrica*, vol. 6 (1938).

J. R. NELSON (ED.), *Marginal Cost Pricing in Practice* (Englewood Cliffs, N.J.: Prentice-Hall, 1964).

RALPH TURVEY, *Optimal Pricing and Investment in Electricity Supply* (London: Allen & Unwin, 1968).

RALPH TURVEY, *Economic Analysis and Public Enterprises* (London: Allen & Unwin, 1971).

RALPH TURVEY (ED.), *Public Enterprise* (Harmondsworth: Penguin, 1968) especially articles by Nancy Ruggles and O. E. Williamson.

Chapter 8

Cost–Benefit Analysis

Chapters 6 and 7 have mentioned the special problems of establishing investment and pricing criteria where, for some reason, financial costs and benefits do not adequately reflect the full consequences of a project. It is to help take account of these 'non-financial' implications that the technique of cost–benefit analysis has been developed, and the brief outline given in this chapter, and the example in Chapter 12, may give the reader some idea of this technique for use in economic appraisal. It can be used in any case where financial returns are an inadequate guide to the real effects of investment, and is particularly suitable if a product is not sold in the market so there is no revenue to give a guide to consumer evaluation (for example in the health and education sectors).

The technique was first developed in the United States in connection with water projects where it was suspected that benefits from such investment would exceed its cost, even though no financial profit was forthcoming (see, for example, Eckstein [1958]). In this case much of the non-financial benefit was in the form of help for isolated communities, and the opportunity for development which adequate water supplies offered. Thus right at the outset cost–benefit analysis (C.B.A.) had to assess benefits which were extremely difficult to quantify.

Its development in this country was similarly fraught with

problems, but some of these have been successively alleviated by its repeated application to a particular field, namely transport. A form of C.B.A. is frequently used by local and central Government in comparing alternative projects, for example schools, hospitals and transport; but the division of money between different areas of investment is often more dependent on political than economic considerations, so C.B.A. is most helpful in determining the relative merits of similar projects, for example different road developments and various sites for a hospital or school. This also minimises the problem of assessing those variables whose quantification is particularly unreliable, such as the value in quality of life (as opposed to standard of living), of having a better-educated population, or the cost of destroyed communities. In comparing projects of different types the evaluation of such factors is likely to play a significant part in the final figures, and so make the conclusions controversial, while the purpose of C.B.A. is to provide as objective as possible a means of making such comparisons. Thus, until much greater agreement is reached on these factors, its main use is likely to be in comparing similar projects or in determining whether such a project shall be undertaken, for which comparisons between different types of costs and benefits are less crucial.

Its most publicised use has been in the decision whether to undertake large investments in the transport field. The first major U. K. analysis was on the costs and benefits of the London–Birmingham motorway (M1) – though the work was not assessed until after it had been built, so this was a retrospective analysis. Similarly an assessment of the new London underground Victoria line was inaugurated mainly to confirm a decision taken on other grounds, though not irrevocably (fortunately both these C.B.A. results indicated that the investments yielded positive net benefits!). However, a prospective analysis of the Fleet underground line was carried out (with similar results) and a highly controversial decision for siting London's third airport was referred to the Roskill Commission for analysis, though in the event the Government decision followed the minority report rather than the Commission's main conclusions. This analysis is described in more detail in Chapter 12, and is a good example of the problems and disagreements which are likely to arise in such a study, and which are mentioned more generally in this chapter.

The theory of cost–benefit analysis is based on a concept already encountered in earlier chapters, that of consumers' surplus. Studies inevitably concentrate rather more on the benefits than the costs, since the latter are often reflected, partially at least, by financial outlays. However, some elements of costs, too, can often be assessed by using the idea of consumers' surplus. The argument is that in a case such as the provision of a new road, each user would be prepared to pay some toll for its use which reflects his valuation of the benefits of travelling by this route rather than the next-best alternative. This is likely to vary for different users, according to the particular journey, the time saved, each man's valuation of his time, and other factors such as income, depreciation of the car and petrol consumption. In the marginal case in which the user is indifferent between his new and old routes, the valuation may be zero, but for most users there will be some positive value put on the opportunity to use the new road. The difference between this value and the price charged (usually zero in this country) is his consumers' surplus, and is a benefit not measured in financial terms. Indeed this applies even if the charge for use is positive, as in the underground investment studies where a charge is levied for journeys undertaken, but this does not always reflect the marginal valuation of benefits for all consumers and all journeys. Demand for transport differs from that usually presented in classic economic analysis because opportunities for its use are, by nature, rather limited. Thus, while oranges may be bought until the marginal utility of their consumption decreases to their price, an individual traveller is likely to make all or none of his journeys on a particular route if this is cheaper or more convenient. However, individual demand discontinuities will be less marked when they are reflected in an aggregate demand curve, and demand may be more elastic in the long run as a new pattern of living and working develops in response to a changed transport situation; and, even in the short run, additional shopping expeditions, for example, may be made if there are better or cheaper transport facilities. In general, however, transport is likely to be 'consumed' in fairly large, discrete and inflexible units because the marginal utility of journeys for different purposes varies so much, so that small variations in demand to bring about equality between marginal utility and price are unlikely.

Another characteristic of transport studies is that the effects of investment are likely to go far beyond just the users of a particular road or underground line; for example, some travellers from London to Birmingham who did not use the new motorway may have benefited from less-crowded roads and trains, just as travellers on older underground lines and bus routes might benefit from a decrease in congestion when some passengers transferred to the Victoria line. And costs, too, may arise for those not directly concerned with the investment under consideration; owners of transport cafes and garages along the old London–Birmingham route are likely to suffer a decline in business as vehicles switch to the motorway, and so lose revenue on capital investment which cannot be moved to more profitable sites. One of the major practical problems of C.B.A. is deciding just how far such effects should be followed up and included in the final calculations. Clearly the 'ripples on the pond' of the economy resulting from the investment have to be ignored beyond a certain point since the problem would otherwise become quite intractable. But how far to follow these effects is almost as difficult to decide as just what value should be placed on each effect.

An extension of how far to follow the effects of any course of action is also important in a wider philosophical context, though not often discussed in practice – namely, how to define and delimit the community whose welfare is being considered. Indeed this is an issue which affects the whole of welfare economics. The unit usually chosen for this purpose is the state or nation, and in practice this is probably the only sensible group of people to consider, simply because this is the largest political unit which wields significant influence. In some contexts, for example in determining common policies in the European Economic Community, several countries may attempt to reach agreements to the mutual benefit of all citizens. Even in this situation, however, negotiators are likely to base their discussion on the interests of their fellow-countrymen who elected or appointed them as representatives. However, a philanthropist might prefer to take a wider view – to consider the good of humanity as a whole for example. Such an approach is appealing in many ways, but because of political constraints it is difficult to see how the concept of 'welfare maximisation' can be extended beyond the state. It should be recognised, however, that the constraints arise in practice rather than in principle, and that there is no automatic principle which decrees that it is the implications of a project for the citizens of a particular country which are paramount.

We have already noted that the valuation of benefits is likely to vary between consumers according to their circumstances. However, it would clearly be an impossible task to identify and interview all potential users of an investment product, and those otherwise affected, and ask them to assess its subjective benefit; some are still children and some not yet born, and even those in a position to quantify the benefits would probably find great difficulty in doing so sensibly. Thus the cost–benefit study must somehow assess the numbers affected in various ways and find an average benefit or cost whereby they evaluate the effect on them. Then all the effects can be combined to see whether or not the result is a positive net benefit.

However, this immediately recalls some of the theoretical issues raised in the first four chapters, for averaging and adding costs and benefits in this way blatantly implies that interpersonal comparisons of welfare are feasible. In effect this method involves directly comparing such effects as a monetary valuation of time saved by consumers with the costs of communities disrupted by a new road. Even if we were only comparing monetary effects (say petrol saved by motorists and reduced profits to garage owners on the old route), this would imply that some interpersonal comparisons are possible, quite contrary to the neoclassicists' original objective of avoiding such exercises. Indeed cost–benefit analysis basically involves Kaldor's compensation criterion, since it rests on the assumption that if the gainers could compensate the losers from their benefit and remain better off (that is self-estimated benefits exceed costs), then the project should be undertaken. The approach also embodies an implication that the distribution of income is satisfactory, since the valuation of a benefit depends, among other things, upon the income of the person receiving it, and in general an individual will value a cost or benefit more highly if he has a large income (at least if we measure in terms of the compensation he would require or be prepared to pay to leave himself in the same position as before). It is important to realise these assumptions used in C.B.A. before becoming too involved in the mechanics of calculation, for it is a significant aspect to examine before judging the validity of the conclusions. In most cases the desire to achieve some measure of costs and benefits will lead us to accept some such assumptions, but there may be cases, for example where a particularly poor section of the community suffers for the benefit of the rich, in which apparent net benefit is not sufficient to ensure the approval of a project. Here we might wish to see some of the compensation paid over by redistributing incomes or paying specific compensation fees before the project could be endorsed. And such a situation may often arise, for most large investment projects, especially in transport, are mainly for the benefit of the better-off members of society who have more facilities for enjoying them. Care must be taken in such cases to see that if poor members of the community bear a large part of the costs, this redistribution of welfare, contrary to the direction which most citizens would wish, is taken into account and if possible reversed. Similarly society usually tries to protect any individual or group of people (rich or poor) from bearing a large burden from an investment for the good of society as a whole, and those in danger of suffering excessive noise nuisance, for example, are often offered some form of compensation.

Some of the problems encountered in cost–benefit analysis arise in any investment project and have already been mentioned in Chapter 6, but they may have special significance in the C.B.A. context. One is how to deal properly with uncertainty, for C.B.A. typically is applied to large one-off projects where there is little experience of how it will change people's patterns of living; often, too, the financial costs escalate considerably from the first estimates. However, some of the problems which would be faced by industry are avoided since bankruptcy is not an issue; a disastrous investment, though a waste of the community's resources, is unlikely to have repercussions on the structure of the establishment. Many of the facets of uncertainty discussed in the previous chapter, and relevant to the more general investment situation, are particularly important in cost–benefit analysis, with the additional problem that even if, say, time saved can be estimated with certainty, its monetary valuation remains controversial. Thus there is the double uncertainty of estimating the exact effects of a project and then converting them to monetary terms. In this case the sensitivity analysis seems particularly appropriate, in which lower and upper limits of the effects and their monetary values can be 'fed in', and changes in critical variables examined. There may sometimes be an opportunity to cancel or alter the project if, as planning proceeds, it becomes clear that the previous values assumed are unsuitable, and a sensitivity analysis should help in such a realignment of an investment. Sensitivity analysis is also likely to be a useful instrument in trying to include 'political objectives' in an assessment where it is difficult to obtain specific valuations of these objectives from the politicians. For example, the balance of payments is often cited as an important factor in investment decisions (usually export increases are considered to be worth more than their monetary value) but it is difficult to find just what weight the Government would attach to its improvement and its importance in different economic conditions. What may be possible, though, is to obtain maximum and minimum values that would be considered reasonable and to use these in a sensitivity analysis. This is clearly the best way to assess a project when precise monetary values are difficult to determine, and enables constructive discussion of the problems and issues involved.

A particular form of uncertainty which often occurs in projects subjected to cost–benefit analysis is what terminal value to place on assets, for typically these projects are long-lasting, and involve investment which theoretically may never deteriorate. This occurred in the Victoria line study where the length of life assumed for tunnels affected the result; yet there is no reason why such investments should ever 'wear out', and in this case it was more a question of ascertaining when they would become technically or commercially obsolete. The only reasonable course seems to be resorting again to sensitivity analysis, using different assessments of the figures to estimate the effects of various forecasts.

The rate of discount may also have a special relevance in cost–benefit analysis because of the somewhat different nature of investments subject to this technique. The factors which suggest a compromise between the opportunity cost of capital and the social time preference rate depend on the assumption that costs and benefits incur opportunity costs both in the private sector and in consumption, which will be true of most public-sector projects. However, an investment subject to C.B.A. may involve a disproportionate amount of these costs and benefits on the consumption side, particularly the benefits, for it is very often because of the non-monetary nature of the returns that the technique is applied. For example, in a health project nearly all the benefits will be non-monetary, and in a case where there is a straightforward choice between building a hospital and a school because of fund-rationing the opportunity costs, too, may be reckoned chiefly in consumption terms. In such a case a discount rate closer to the S.T.P.R. is likely to be more appropriate than the more general-purpose compromise. (A special case of such an investment decision, though without particular reference to C.B.A., is outlined in Chapter 10.) Some doubt arose in assessing the Victoria line investment about the best rate of interest, and it was found that the two rates used made a considerable difference to the results achieved. Again this type of sensitivity analysis, using different values of variables to assess their results, is probably the most sensible.

The issue of rationing, mentioned in the previous paragraph, gives rise to one of the chief problems of deciding between investments in the public sector. For though in principle projects should be undertaken until the net return is zero, in practice funds are likely to be limited so that some balance between different objectives needs to be achieved; for example, a project with high monetary benefits may be an alternative to one with high non-financial returns. One approach to this issue is to examine past decisions and deduce from these what the relative priorities of Government are, that is to conduct a revealed-preference analysis of official behaviour. This assumes of course that preference patterns have remained reasonably stable over the period of study, an assumption which may well not be true if Governments, or the constraints within which they operate, have changed. A more practical use of the revealed-preference results might be as a basis for further decisions, that is as suggestions to make to decision-makers for alteration where appropriate. Enabling the politician to choose his own final alternatives and their relative value is often easier than asking him to specify an abstract objective function since there is sometimes a political advantage in not defining objectives explicitly. It must also be remembered that, in practice, there is considerable bargaining involved in investment decisions since we are not ruled by a benign dictator but by a group of politicians and a sophisticated bureaucratic machinery. Thus the economist who may be impatient to make certain issues clear may find this is not easy in the context of practical decisions. In this case his task must be to analyse and assist in whatever manner most helps the decision-maker.

However, even within his own analysis the C.B.A. practitioner is likely to encounter problems because of the nature of the projects under consideration. One that occurs particularly with transport investment is the valuation of time saved. In almost any major transport project some travellers will be able to make the same journey in less time, and relief of congestion on the established routes may mean that this applies even to travellers who do not use the new investment directly. Just how to value this time in terms of benefit to the individual is difficult to determine, and a number of writers have made suggestions, including M. E. Beesley [1965], who reconsidered this subject after his participation in the Victoria line study. Time saved on journeys made during working hours was assumed to be valued at the rate per hour paid to the person making the journey, so some average wage of a typical traveller could be used to evaluate these savings. However, the valuation of non-working time saved is much more controversial, and often makes a significant difference to the net benefit of transport investment. Clearly the value of the time saved to the traveller depends partly on his reason for travelling (it is unlikely to be the same for commuters and tourists for example) but the most appropriate figure is hard to determine. Two suggested values were one-third and one-half the average value of working time saved, and the figure used makes a significant difference to the results in many transport studies. As Chapter 12 shows, this was a controversial area in determining the relative merits of sites for London's third airport. Another factor which arises because of reduced congestion is that the comfort of the journey, particularly on public transport, is likely to be improved. Again this is difficult to evaluate, though some trade-off between this and other considerations may be estimated by observing consumers' behaviour. For example, if consumers are prepared to take a longer or more expensive journey to provide them with greater comfort, some idea of relative values can be established. However, any precise or generally accepted figure will be very difficult to ascertain.

One result of many major public investments, especially transport and health projects, is a saving of injury or of life. Some of the most difficult and controversial arguments arise in this area, for the valuing of suffering and of human life is an emotive topic. Protracted court cases for compensation after accidental injury or death indicate just how difficult it is to convert such factors satisfactorily into monetary terms. One objective way of valuing a life from the community's point of view would be to look at the economic contribution its owner would have made to the community had he lived. However, this yields the anomalous result that it would actually be detrimental to save the lives of retirement pensioners whose future life entails consumption but no production; it also omits consideration of the suffering and loss caused to the victim's family and friends. Another approach might be to use the life-insurance policies as a valuation of their own lives by members of the public − though these figures are complicated by the fact that (like most valuations) they depend on income, and they are often used as investments as well as life insurance. Probably some average figure from compensation in the courts would be the best solution, for here the case has been argued carefully before a conclusion is reached. This would only cover the personal aspect of death and injury however; it would be necessary to add on to this some consideration for the cost to the community of lost economic contributions and the expense of treating injuries. Indeed, courts often award a greater sum as compensation to those who are severely disabled than to the survivors of those who are killed. This reflects both the additional costs of care in such cases, and the opportunities available for the reconstruction of the lives of a bereaved family (perhaps by remarriage of the widowed survivor) but not for those who must care for the permanently disabled. Any such attempt to put a value on human life and suffering may seem unduly harsh and callous, and the immediate reaction may be that it cannot be valued, and that life in particular should be saved at all costs. But society does not really practice these values and save life whenever possible – the fact that many people who could be saved by artificial kidneys die each year because there is insufficient money to provide the necessary equipment illustrates this clearly. So a feeling of distaste at valuing these aspects of investment, however understandable, does not reflect society's implied values, nor help to allocate the country's resources most appropriately through choice of the best investment. This is another discussion taken up in more detail in the Roskill Commission study which forms the subject of Chapter 12.

As we shall see, the report on the third London airport also highlights the problems which can arise in evaluating a particular loss – that of communities which may have to be physically destroyed in such a project, or which may gradually disintegrate if their *raison d'être* is affected, for example through being bypassed by a new road. To evaluate such losses is extremely difficult, since they seem to involve a greater penalty to the wider community than would less concentrated adverse effects. However, there seems little alternative to merely summing the individual costs of removal and resettlement, since the 'atmosphere' of a community is clearly beyond monetary interpretation.

This chapter has outlined some of the issues of Government decision-making which are particularly emphasised by cost–benefit analysis projects. Clearly a separate book could be written (and indeed many have been) on this topic, and the problems which are associated with it, and readers may wish to follow these up in one of the books mentioned in the list below. This review has tried to introduce the basic concepts of this investment-appraisal technique and to mention some of the problems likely to be encountered so that the student of welfare economics is aware of how that theory can be used to facilitate policy decisions. Chapter 12 examines in more detail some of the issues which arose in the Roskill Commission's study of the siting of London's third airport, an example of the use of C.B.A. as a decision-making tool by Governments. How the more general aspects of Government public policy have developed since the war is discussed in the next chapter.

Suggestions for Further Reading

M. E. BEESLEY, 'The Value of Time Spent in Travelling: Some New Evidence', *Economica*, vol. 32 (1965).
M. E. BEESLEY AND C. D. FOSTER, 'The Victoria Line: Social Benefits

and Finances', *Journal of the Royal Statistical Society*, series B, vol. 128 (1965).

S. B. CHASE JR (ED.), *Problems in Public Expenditure*, Brookings Institution (London: Allen & Unwin, 1968).

OTTO ECKSTEIN, *Water Resources Development* (Harvard University Press, 1958).

E. J. MISHAN, *Elements of Cost Benefit Analysis* (London: Allen & Unwin, 1972).

D. W. PEARCE, *Cost Benefit Analysis* (London: Macmillan, 1971).

A. R. PREST AND R. TURVEY, 'Cost Benefit Analysis: A Survey', in *Surveys of Economic Thought*, vol. 3 (London: Macmillan, 1966).

J. N. WOLFE (ED.), *Cost Benefit and Cost Effectiveness* (London: Allen & Unwin, 1973) especially articles by Watson and Mansfield and by Alan Williams.

Chapter 9

U. K. Public Policy since 1945

The previous chapters in this part of the book have shown three contexts in which public policy can be applied and developed from the theoretical basis presented in Part One. What this chapter shows is how U.K. Governments have developed a policy for the public sector since 1945 and the extent to which these have coincided with the principles suggested in previous chapters. This should help the reader to acquire some perspective of the issues, so that the ideas previously developed in a somewhat abstract setting can be seen against the historical and institutional constraints which in practice limit their application in the United Kingdom.

Public sectors are found in economies differing widely in structure and philosophy, and their exact role in each case is closely related to the context in which they are set. In communist countries most economic assets are collectively owned and organised and the administration of the public sector is synonymous with that of the whole economy. There are virtually no societies now without any publicly owned assets, but there are many economies in which the public sector is kept to its minimum size, involving perhaps only provision for external and internal security which is difficult to meet through private enterprise. The appropriate Government attitude to the public sector depends partly on its size and history of development as well as the political atmosphere of the country. Thus it is helpful in understanding U.K. policy to have some idea of the history of nationalised industries in the United Kingdom.

Most of the present nationalised industries were taken into public ownership under the 1945–51 Labour Government, and though the exact reasoning behind each nationalisation was not made explicit, most industries fulfil one or more of three criteria (though these are not always distinct). The first was a philosophical principle: the Labour Party had been committed to increasing public ownership, and certain key industries were evidently appropriate for extending Government influence in the economy. The steel, fuel and transport industries all lay in this field, as did the Bank of England which had been under Government control for many years before its official nationalisation in 1946. In the steel and coal industries, particularly, the possibility of a different attitude to employment policy than had been exercised under private ownership was probably a significant factor in nationalisation. Another reason to extend public ownership was associated with reconstructing the post-war economy. The war (and the pre-war depression) had left many key industries badly underinvested, and considerable finance was needed to revitalise them, capital which private enterprise would have had great difficulty in raising at a time when a shortage of consumer goods was placing serious pressure on the country's resources. The railways in particular needed a large injection of capital to replace worn and obsolete fixed equipment and rolling stock. The third reason for nationalising some industries was the need for rationalisation within them which could only sensibly be carried out by a single owner; state monopoly was thought to be preferable to private control and the power this might place in the hands of owners of key sectors. The most obvious examples in this category were the gas and electricity industries which had previously been owned by a large number of public and private firms of varying sizes. Many of the industries nationalised after the war belonged to more than one of these categories for public ownership, as the following list of the main industries (not in the order nationalised) brought under public control at that time suggests: the Bank of England, road transport, railways, air transport, most canals, coal, gas and electricity, and steel. The public-sector industries incorporated after the war have remained largely unchanged apart from the denationalisation of steel and road transport in 1951, the renationalisation of steel in 1967 and the progressive public control of road passenger transport in the 1960s and 1970s. Rolls-Royce was nationalised in 1972, the British National Oil Company was instituted in 1975, and there is now (1976) a plan for public ownership of much of the aero industry. However, these developments have been largely incidental to the development of over-all public-sector policy, and have not, so far, radically affected Government policy towards established nationalised industries; this has developed a remarkably consistent pattern through several changes of Government since the war.

This chapter concentrates on that part of the public sector whose products are sold to consumers. Of course there are other parts, mainly providing services, and a large proportion of the public sector produces output which is distributed as far as possible according to individual need and financed on a criterion of ability to pay. These parts of the public sector differ from nationalised industries in two important respects: they do not, ostensibly at least, form part of the market system for resource allocation, since their provision depends on other criteria; they may also face private competition (from which some nationalised industries are statutorily protected), as do the health and education sectors for example. This part of the public sector was also largely developed and established in the early post-war years (for example the universal system of free education following the 1944 Education Act and the National Health Service set up in 1948), and clearly in this case the main arguments for public provision were philosophical ideas based on socialist principles. Some parts of the public sector have of course been nationally owned for much longer; the Post Office was a Government department from its inception in the nineteenth century to its establishment as a Corporation in 1970, and the armed forces have been paid and equipped from some form of public taxation since the Middle Ages. Those parts of the public sector which do not sell goods or services to the public on a market basis are clearly of a different kind from those which do — and so Government policy towards them is different. There is, for example, no question of 'revenues covering costs', since the consumers do not necessarily pay for the product. This means that pricing policy is irrelevant, and investment policy therefore takes on a more important and less easily defined role, since the wishes of consumers cannot be ascertained from their willingness to pay. Chapters 6 and 8 have outlined some of the difficulties which arise in the economic planning of such industries, and have suggested some possible solutions. But most of the discussion on public-sector policy has centred on the role which nationalised industries should play, and particularly on the criteria by which private and nationalised industries should be judged in a mixed economy.

The obvious place to start looking for such guidelines is in the Nationalisation Acts themselves. These differ considerably in detail according to the nature of the industry and assets concerned, but in the principles laid down for their operation certain themes are common, and three main objectives emerge (for example, see *Gas Act* [1948]). One is that the industries bear some responsibility for fostering the welfare of their employees, though no specific guidelines for this end are suggested. Another statutory obligation is that there should be no 'undue discrimination' between consumers in pricing the product, though since no elaboration of the meaning of this phrase is given, it may seem a somewhat ambiguous directive. The nationalised industries were also obliged to see that revenues were sufficient to cover costs 'taking one year with another' so no cost or credit to the Exchequer was anticipated from the day-to-day running of the industries. Thus the public sector was given responsibilities to three parts of the community – to its employees, to its consumers and to the general public as owners – by covering costs. Exactly how it should embody these obligations within daily policy, or reconcile them if they were mutually contradictory, was not suggested.

The interpretation of these principles in the immediate post-nationalisation period was not considered controversial. For many of the industries the prime task was to boost investment and output to meet the needs of the post-war economy, and the Treasury supplied the funds, leaving the nationalised industries largely autonomous in their requirement to earn sufficient revenue to cover running costs and interest on loans and payment to previous owners. Each industry was vested in a Corporation with a Chairman and Board to lay down the principles of management, and Government interference in day-to-day matters was minimal. Thus, apart from the upheaval caused by the change of Government and denationalisation of most of the steel and road transport industries in 1951, and various bodies set up to look after passenger transport, the public sector was left largely to its own devices for a decade.

However in the late 1950s and early 1960s the relative independence of the nationalised industries was interrupted by the coincidence of several heavy demands on the Treasury for investment funds. These arose at this time to finance both new and replacement investment. Changing technology presented many new opportunities for investment, and the depreciation on assets used by the public sector had been on a historic basis; nationalised industries typically own a large proportion of long-lasting assets, so their replacement after twenty or thirty years is likely to be a great deal more expensive than their original cost, which was all that depreciation allowances provided. At the same time, the industries were wanting not just to replace but to improve machinery, and the post-war growth in technology provided a number of opportunities for this. The railways, which had not really succeeded in covering costs satisfactorily since the war, wanted to streamline the services and extend electrification and signalling equipment on several commuter and inter-city routes. The coal industry, after its initial effort to meet heavy post-war demand, now wanted to rationalise its operations and introduce sophisticated underground equipment into the more profitable mines. The electricity industry was anticipating a further substantial rise in demand, and was considering building large conventional generating units as well as embarking on a nuclear-energy programme. Similarly the gas industry, which had faced stagnant demand since the war, wanted to invest in more efficient methods of coal gasification, and later in a new oil-gasification process. All these demands led to considerable pressure on the Treasury and the taxpayer and, not surprisingly, to some Government reflection on the role and management of nationalised industries.

The result of these thoughts was published in 1961 as a White Paper called *The Financial and Economic Obligations of the Nationalised Industries*. It appeared during a Conservative Government, but its main recommendations were later endorsed by the Labour Party when it came to power in 1964. As far as the three obligations (to employees, consumers and public owners) were concerned, this document was mainly concerned with the latter, that is obligations to taxpayers in ensuring that revenue was adequate, though these criteria also involved the consumer by affecting the prices charged and, indirectly, employees in determining investment guidelines. (However, the responsibility for the welfare of employees had diminished in importance during this period of low unemployment, except in the coal industry where widespread redundancy of skilled and specialised workers, who were not easy to redeploy, was recognised as a special problem.) The two main recommendations of the report were to suggest that some allowance be made to cover the difference between depreciating at historic and replacement cost and to institute a system of financial targets for each industry.

Depreciation is an accounting rather than an economic tool. Accountants must consider depreciation on all past investment whereas the economist is concerned with equipment wearing out only when this brings forward the date at which it must be replaced. Nevertheless the accounting and economic concepts are related, as was suggested in Chapter 7, and depreciating assets which will have to be renewed at replacement cost rather that at the cost at which they were bought (possibly decades previously) clearly brings the accounting techniques more into line with the ideas of economic investment appraisal. This move was primarily instigated to reduce pressure on Treasury funds, but it incidentally made more sense in the economic allocation of resources.

The role of the financial targets was rather more ambiguous. They were calculated individually for each industry to reflect particular conditions of supply and demand, and were usually expressed as a net return on net assets. Each target was to cover a five-year period (the first one was 1962–7 in most cases) and its value was set after discussions between each industry and the sponsoring Ministry. The motive for introducing targets was undoubtedly to provide funds for the industries to finance some of their own investment, thus reducing the pressure on the Treasury. Whether they were supposed to reflect some consistent pricing and investment policy, or were merely calculated from agreed forecasts of demand and costs at present trends and practices, was not made clear. It seems likely that the latter was the case and the financial targets were introduced as an incentive to management to increase efficiency rather than as an opportunity to impose particular economic principles. The consequences of failure to achieve the target return were not made clear, and in practice many of the industries did not achieve either the first or second quinquennial targets because other aspects of economic and social policy intervened.

It is interesting to examine the effect on prices which a five-year target return on net assets may have. One clear temptation if the target return has not been achieved in the early years is to increase prices just before the end of a quinquennium in order to boost profits. (This situation might arise from bad forecasting of demand, unexpected increases in costs or a general change in economic conditions.) Thus prices may become out of line with costs even if the targets are set on the basis of sensible pricing policy, for prices would have to cover past shortfalls in the target, as well as bringing revenues and costs into the appropriate relation for targets to be reached in the future. This problem is aggravated in the case of some nationalised industries which need to give consumers several months' notice of price changes (for example gas, electricity and telephone services). Thus if such an industry wants to increase revenue during the subsequent year, price changes cannot be implemented until three or four months later, and so a year's revenue must be recouped in only nine or eight months. These factors have two undesirable effects on prices: one quite clearly is to raise them above the general level which targets are meant to reflect, and, if this is based on the optimal allocation of resources, to distort the level of prices which determine consumers' expenditure; there may also be public-relations difficulties with consumers facing a steep rise in prices at the end of each quinquennium.

The solution to the problems inherent in five-year targets is not easy to find. To make targets annual would not allow for trading fluctuations which are bound to occur in some years, and in any case there might still be a rush to increase prices at the end of the year. To extend targets beyond five years would exacerbate many of the problems already encountered, and it is difficult to make reasonable forecasts of costs and demand for periods of longer than five years, so that the basis on which the target was originally set might become irrelevant. One possibility is to make targets more flexible, so they could be amended during the quinquennium if circumstances warranted such a course and keeping to the target would involve serious misallocation of resources. The difficulty is that this could involve Ministers in the affairs of nationalised industries to an increasing extent if the target were to be continuously subject to review, thus demoralising the management of the industries who might feel they were not being given sufficient responsibility. Even if more interference did not result from such a scheme, an industry whose target was changed frequently might feel that it had no clear management objective, and standards of efficiency could suffer as a result.

This raises a question of the status of a target as an incentive to management efficiency, an issue already mentioned in earlier chapters. Clearly management must have some guide as to the level of returns which can be expected in the absence of a free-market situation where profits are an indication of efficiency. Some economists suggest that the target should be set rather higher than can reasonably be expected, to keep management 'up to the mark'. However, this would raise additional problems: in aiming to achieve this 'too-high' target, management may put prices above the level which Government considers desirable; or in time the nationalised industries may come to realise that the targets are not necessarily meant to be realistic and so regard them as the maximum achievement level rather than as a 'normal' or minimum target. It has been claimed that the morale of management in public-sector industries is an important factor of efficiency, and that in industries which make a loss, morale is likely to suffer. This seems to be primarily a result of general and Government attitude towards losses in the public sector, for clearly if it is generally thought that losses indicate inefficiency, then they are bound to have a bad effect on morale. However, if it is made clear from the start that Government policy involves some nationalised industries making losses, and some being less profitable than others, then it becomes management's job to see that the policies are carried out with maximum efficiency, that is minimum loss for those policies (analysis in Chapter 3 has shown that the optimal resource-allocation policy may involve deficits if it comprises marginal-cost pricing in decreasing-cost industries). In such a case there is no need for management to feel it has 'failed' because costs exceed revenue, as long as others do not consider this a sign of failure.

Some of the problems of setting targets in the form proposed in the 1961 White Paper were well illustrated when the gas industry had to adjust to the technological changes involved in exploiting the North Sea reserves, a problem which is discussed in some detail in Chapter 10. First it was faced with substantial investment in distribution equipment, both to provide a national grid for North Sea gas and to strengthen existing pipes for the higher pressure under which natural gas is pumped. At the same time a substantial conversion programme for consumers' appliances was needed, so that considerable expenditure was involved. However, the effect of much of this investment was to increase the assets of the industry by adding to those which would not be productive for several years; expressing a financial target as a net return on net assets effectively increased the revenue needed by the gas industry in a period when substantial investment which showed no immediate returns was necessary. Similarly 'writing off' assets (as has been done in the railway industry) automatically reduces the amount of revenue needed to achieve a target 'return on assets'. Thus variations of this kind may change quite drastically the pricing and investment criteria inherent in achieving a target set without due consideration of such circumstances.

The gas industry's target was affected differently after the initial investment was complete and exploitation of North Sea gas was under way. Because the gas industry possesses monopsony power over the oil companies and monopoly power in the market, the economic rent arising from the ownership of reserves of natural gas is taken directly by the gas industry rather than by the central Government. This would not make any difference so long as the financial target of the gas industry was adjusted to take account of this advantage or the increased profit returned to the Government. However, if the financial target is left at its previous value, the gas industry will be able to meet it more easily, and so may set prices below the level originally incorporated in the target, or may become lax in management. A better system, it is suggested, would be to auction the rights of exploration so that the Government reaps the rent from the resources and for the gas industry to buy at marginal cost (including cost of exploration rights) from the oil companies (Dam [1964]). Then the rent would go straight to the Government without any being lost by possible gas industry inefficiency. It is very difficult to prove or disprove that efficiency is affected by such factors, but there seems no reason inherent in the institutional framework of targets which would lead to adverse effects on the efficiency of nationalised industries. However, it does provide another example in which flexibility of targets with changing conditions is necessary if they are truly to reflect the Government's public-sector policies.

As well as financial targets, more specific investment reviews were introduced after the 1961 White Paper. These served a double purpose in giving the sponsoring Minister some insight into the problems and constraints of each industry, and provided an opportunity for discussion of the Government's long-term proposals for the industry. It can also give the Government a sanction against nationalised industries so that if they do not toe the line, the Government may not be co-operative at the next investment review. It seems desirable that nationalised industries and Government should review investment proposals together, although Government objectives for the industries should be formalised as far as possible and then direct interference kept to a minimum; for the management of the nationalised industries, though subject to Government policy, is more likely to know the best business practices in various circumstances, and undue Government interference may hamper its commercial judgement. Joint investment reviews are clearly important and valuable, however, and correct and consistent investment decisions are a vital base to forming a pricing policy, as we have seen in Chapters 6 and 7.

A target rate of return on new investment was also introduced somewhat later – originally at 8 per cent and later raised to 10 per cent. Any investment undertaken by nationalised industries was to provide a positive net present value when discounted at this rate (or show an internal rate of return at this level or above). Thus the return on assets approved under this scheme should be at least the target investment rate, and under conditions where the provision of all assets had been on such a basis, and no errors had been made in forecasting costs and demand, the achieved rate of return on all assets should be the same as the test discount rate used. In practice life is not so simple, for example there may be obsolete equipment which because of unforeseen changes does not earn the target rate of return. Some new investment, for example the provision of the natural gas grid, may meet the investment criterion in the long run, but not necessarily in the first few years of its life when it is not fully productive. Because of such problems two targets are needed – one on future investment, which should include social considerations where applicable, and one on total assets which takes account of historic influences on the industry. These two targets are provided by the test discount rate and the financial objective.

The Government (this time a Labour administration) revised the 1961 White Paper in 1967 when it published *Nationalised Industries: A Review of Economic and Financial Objectives*. This was largely to resolve some problems of principle which had arisen since 1961, and continued a slow move towards marginal-cost pricing which had existed during the 1960s. When the 1961 White Paper was published the implied pricing policy was one of 'average cost plus', that is revenues should be sufficient to cover average running costs and meet the financial target. Some industries, particularly gas, electricity and railways, used multi-part tariffs, largely as a commercial gambit to encourage the widest use of fixed assets. The importance of pricing as a resource-allocation tool really only emerged explicitly after the 1961 White Paper had been published and mainly under the 1964–70 Labour Government. A number of policy documents developed this theme – the 1965 *National Plan* emphasised 'the role of public sector policy in minimising overall costs', and in the same year a White Paper on *Fuel Policy* took an ambiguous attitude, recommending that a movement towards marginal-cost pricing should take place but emphasising the importance of achieving an adequate return on all investment, past and present. Inherent ambiguities in such a recommendation were not resolved, nor even acknowledged. Gradually a view seemed to be emerging that marginal-cost pricing was a 'good thing' for resource allocation, but politicians shied away from over-enthusiasm because of the implications of deficits in decreasing-cost industries. Explicit justifications for the principle of such a pricing policy are difficult to find, but its place in Government publications became gradually established. The 1967 White Paper faced more honestly some of the problems which might emerge.

The Government's policy ... starts from the principle that nationalised industries should normally cover their accounting costs in full – including the service of capital and appropriate provision for its replacement. But important though this is, it is not in itself sufficient to produce a rational pricing policy. Prices, if they are to contribute towards a more efficient distribution of resources, must also attract resources to places where they can make the most effective contribution to meeting the demands of users.

The paper goes on to make it clear that it considers the last task is best achieved by marginal-cost pricing, though with little consideration of the arguments and counter-arguments presented earlier in this book.

The 1967 White Paper also throws more light on the official attitude to the financial targets.

Clear financial objectives . . . serve both as an incentive to management and as one of the standards by which success or failure . . . may be judged . . . the Government will take into account (in setting objectives) the considerations – return on new investment, soundly based pricing policy, social obligations, conditions of demand, domestic costs and other factors peculiar to the individual undertaking.

Further comments show that the Government realises that this attitude implies different targets for different industries, and that targets may have to be amended if circumstances change unexpectedly. Thus the official attitude at this time, at least in principle, seems to be the same as that suggested earlier in this chapter as the best role for financial targets.

A 1969 White Paper – *Ministerial Control of the Nationalised Industries* – also helped explain the Government's attitude towards financial targets. Here it was quite explicitly stated that the 'financial objectives should become the financial expression of the pricing and investment criteria already laid down', though there was little clarification of previous ambiguous statements on what these should be. However, the Government did comment on the proposal that official pricing policy should be made statutory for the nationalised industries, and this raised the question to what extent it is desirable and practicable for the Government to dictate required price levels. Clearly the nationalised industries must be able to vary prices to some extent according to commercial circumstances (for example it would be inappropriate to force either the gas or electricity industries to charge for connection of new homes if its competitor persists in subsidising these services), and in any case there will be some exceptions to the marginal-cost-pricing rule where unavoidable price distortions or social costs cause the best attainable policy to be one which diverges from marginal-cost pricing. Marginal-cost pricing should include social costs in the calculations, but the present institutional framework of nationalised industries involves them in considering only their own private costs. Where these differ from social costs, the Government should direct that social aspects be included in prices, and this may mean a move away from prices reflecting private marginal costs. In any case it would not be feasible for a Minister to check that statutory price policies were being implemented without considerable interference in the industry. It would seem better for the Government to make known its pricing and investment policies, reflect these in the financial targets, and encourage their application by informal contacts between the sponsoring Ministry and the industry.

However, it is clear from the various official papers published in the late 1960s that no clear pricing policy did emerge. The contradiction between average- and marginal-cost pricing was never adequately resolved. Let us re-examine the theoretical case for each policy. Both can be justified on welfare grounds: average-cost pricing because there is no transfer of welfare; marginal-cost pricing because it enables the individual to allocate resources in the optimum way for the economy as a whole in choosing what is best for himself. It has been shown that in an industry with decreasing average costs, marginal-cost pricing means an accounting loss, and hence subsidy of that industry's consumers by the general taxpayer. This does not seem untoward in a system for which taxation is an important instrument of social justice, and in which some members of society are largely subsidised from public funds (students and pensioners for example). The argument that subsidies would weaken the morale of the industries is valid only so long as the public, and particularly the Government, consider the need for such subsidies to be a sign of inefficiency. What is really needed is a clear understanding of what the Government's pricing objectives are, and financial targets designed to reflect these and sensible investment decisions. To obtain explicit statements of such investment and pricing policies has not, however, proved easy in the past. We have already seen that the Government felt the nationalised industries should play a number of roles not always compatible, but made little attempt to provide a formula or guidance for reconciling them. Reconciliation of this sort is an area which economists have traditionally avoided, laying responsibility for the weighting of different objectives at the door of the politicians – and it is indeed difficult to see how anyone except the elected Government has the right to balance the respective merits of, say, resource allocation and a prices-and-incomes policy, or decide what are the social costs of untreatable pollution. However, the Government itself has not been very articulate in laying down guidelines, and it has fallen to official non-Government bodies faced with particular problems to attempt a reconciliation of incompatible objectives. One body which did attempt this rather thankless task was the National Board for Prices and Incomes (P.I.B.).

The P.I.B., established in 1965 to implement the Government's prices-and-incomes policy, looked at a number of nationalised industries before it was disbanded in 1971, and it is interesting to note its own interpretation of its purpose. It was established primarily as an anti-inflation weapon to identify permissible increases in prices and incomes, using for guidance the *Prices and Incomes Policy*. However, the P.I.B. itself took the following view: 'It is the change in the practical world of the nature of the competitive process which in our view dictates the need for a prices and incomes policy' [1968]. The Board saw itself as providing a replacement for that process and in so doing set itself two main tasks – to encourage marginal-cost pricing (on the grounds of its occurrence in competitive markets rather than directly for welfare reasons) and to increase management efficiency, which may have inadequate incentive in non-competitive markets. It is unfortunate that the P.I.B. was never given the opportunity to comment on how financial targets should fit into their concept of providing a substitute for competition, since this was also an instrument to encourage a consistent pricing policy as well as efficiency. All references on public-sector prices and incomes were given on the understanding that financial targets must be met, and though the Board asked for an opportunity to comment on them this was never provided. The P.I.B. was particularly concerned that prices should reflect social costs where these differed from private costs, and one of their studies, on the resource costs of employing miners, is discussed in Chapter 13.

Government attitude to the public sector since 1970 has not been very clear. The Conservative Government elected in that year stated their intention of selling back to private industry at least some profitable nationalised-industry activities, and a few of the Coal Board's peripheral trading interests were offered to shareholders. However, the policy was not executed to any significant extent, and little was heard of it after 1971. The return of a minority Labour Government in 1974 again aroused a tendency to strong doctrinaire statements, and talk of nationalising leading firms as soon as possible, though this was never enshrined in official Government statements. At present further nationalisation plans seem to be largely in the shipbuilding and aerospace industries and the gradual development of the British National Oil Company to take an interest in North Sea oil exploitation. As far as pricing and investment policies are concerned, the main Government guidelines seem to be that the nationalised industries should become profitable again as soon as possible after the recent heavy losses. (Most industries failed to meet their first two quinquennial targets, and these were not reset for a third period in which anti-inflation policies became paramount.) The prime consideration at present, then, seems to be to charge at least average-cost prices in the nationalised industries, though the present structure of multi-part tariffs suggests this might be an acceptable compromise so long as total costs are covered. No doubt marginal-cost pricing in a constant-cost industry would be acceptable (in any case it would coincide with average-cost prices) but there seems little emphasis on the microeconomic principles of organising nationalised industries; probably either a substantial surplus or deficit would be politically unpopular. It is rather the macroeconomic role which the public sector can play in keeping prices low which has increasingly occupied Government policy in the last decade, even at the risk of misallocating resources between the public and private sectors. The resolution of over-all responsibility to the economy, and individual role within the economic system, has been neglected here and in many similar discussions. However, it does not lend itself easily to economic analysis, so that the best approach seems to be that suggested earlier in this part of the book, and particularly in Chapter 8. Post-war Governments themselves seem loathe to tackle the problem of competing objectives, so their views can only be deduced from decisions in practice. Part Three gives four examples of such decisions which illustrate not only the welfare principles derived in Part One but also some of the problems which their implementation may involve.

Suggestions for Further Reading

DAVID COOMBES, *State Enterprise,* Political and Economic Planning (London: Allen & Unwin, 1971).

K. W. DAM, 'Oil and Gas Licensing in the North Sea', *Journal of Law and Economics,* vol. 7 (1964).

H.M. GOVERNMENT, *The Financial and Economic Obligations of the Nationalised Industries,* Cmnd. 1337 (London: H.M.S.O., 1961).

H.M. GOVERNMENT, *Nationalised Industries: A Review of Economic and Financial Objectives,* Cmnd. 3437 (London: H.M.S.O., 1967).

RICHARD PRYKE, *Public Enterprise in Practice: The British Experience of Nationalisation over Two Decades* (London: MacGibbon & Kee, 1971).

G. L. REID AND K. ALLEN, *Nationalised Industries* (Harmondsworth: Penguin, 1970).

G. L. REID, K. ALLEN AND D. J. HARRIS, *The Nationalised Fuel Industries* (London: Heinemann, 1973).

Part Three

Practice – Some Examples

Chapter 10

Exploiting the United Kingdom's Oil Reserves

This last part of the book gives four examples of practical issues in which the principles developed in earlier chapters are relevant to policy decisions. In the following three chapters the cases quoted have all been subject to lengthy discussion, and in two instances to official reports, so that they can be examined to shed some light on how Government may view the decisions and compromises it has to make. The subject of this chapter, however, is a less well established one, so that in this case the discussion takes the form mainly of posing questions rather than suggesting solutions.

The discovery of extensive oil reserves beneath the North Sea has revolutionised the United Kingdom's pattern of fuel supply, and has changed, at least for a couple of decades, the constraints which have traditionally surrounded this sector of the economy. The coincidence of these finds with the rapidly rising world price of oil in the early 1970s, which made their exploitation commercially viable, seemed providential. But as with any endowment they bring with them responsibilities to use the reserves to the best advantage of U.K. citizens and their descendants, and the solution of these considerations is not altogether straightforward. Probably the most important decision to be made is the optimum time and rate of its use, and in this form the problem highlights several issues already discussed, including the most appropriate rate of discount, the difficulty of allowing for the divergence of private and social costs and how to deal with uncertainty.

To illustrate the relevance of these factors a brief review of the history of North Sea operations may be helpful. Licences to explore and exploit sections of the North Sea were originally granted in the expectation that the chief discovery would be gas; the exploring companies (usually oil consortia) were granted licences for a nominal fee, according to how fast they intended to explore and on the understanding that all gas found (except when intended for certain chemical processes) should be offered to the Gas Council (now the British Gas Corporation). However, the discovery of commercial quantities of oil, which is retailed chiefly through private companies, raised a slightly different issue. For whereas the gas industry, as a monopsonist buyer from the North Sea and monopolist retailer, can set its own price for gas discoveries (as long as it covers the costs of exploitation and normal profit to induce the drilling companies to continue operations) in selling direct to retailers, the chief determinant of oil price is 'what the market will pay'. In a competitive industry with a perfectly elastic supply of factors of production no problem arises since supply and demand are in equilibrium at a price which ensures equality between consumers' marginal utility and cost of production. But two factors in North Sea oil operations frustrate such an equilibrium. There is in any case only a limited amount of oil available so that there is likely to be an economic rent accruing to those fortunate enough to be able to exploit it; and the high risks and heavy capital expenditure required exclude many small firms from the market. Production constraints imposed by a particular tax regime, weather conditions and the need for good oil-field practice also yield economic rents to some producers. This means that the system is not perfectly competitive, and there is no market mechanism which will ensure that the rate of depletion and equilibrium price of oil will maximise welfare in the fuel market or in the wider community. Hence arises the need for Government intervention and policy in this area.

One problem in determining the best approach is that any fuel policy is intimately involved with general economic development. The main determinant of demand for energy is the general level of economic activity, since this affects both the needs of industry and the disposable incomes of private citizens. Similarly there cannot be a large increase in industrial activity unless there are adequate fuel supplies to support it. Thus anticipating the need for fuel involves careful forecasting of real rates of economic growth. Demand for energy as a whole depends mainly on factors other than price, so that it is relatively price-inelastic. However, since each fuel has a substitute in most uses, individual fuel demand is fairly responsive to changes in relative prices, at least in the long run when new equipment can be bought. Despite this general competitiveness, different fuels are more appropriate by their nature and price for different functions (for example gas and electricity for domestic markets, coal and oil for non-specialist industrial use), and to take account of all these factors a reiterative model of the economy must be constructed in which fuel needs, supplies, costs, prices and elasticities are considered together to ensure a consistent result. Such forecasting is far from easy at a distance of twenty or thirty years, and the consequences of significant errors may be quite serious for resource allocation.

Other unknowns also complicate the search for an ideal solution. One of the most basic factors, the extent of recoverable reserves, is itself uncertain, and the proportion of reserves which can be exploited may increase from the present 20 to 25 per cent as technology advances. Estimates of total oil available can be made from what is known of reserves and other countries' finds in the North Sea, but these cannot be an adequate substitute for knowledge of how much oil is available. How long reserves last depends not only on the original extent of reserves but also on the rate of exploitation, and these two factors are strongly interdependent. For large estimates of reserves reduce the apparent need for conservation, and so may lead to rapid depletion in the early years, just as an under-estimate of total oil available would lead to a postponement of its use so that less is consumed in the immediate future than welfare maximisation would indicate. However, it is interesting to note that the depletion decision is asymmetric, since a conservative exploitation rate can be accelerated, albeit with some delay for production adjustments, while it may be impossible to reverse a rapid depletion policy once it is under way. This is a case where the sensitivity analysis suggested in Chapter 6 would highlight the implications of each investment decision.

If marginal-cost pricing is used with consistent investment criteria, it will ensure that demand and supply are balanced in the long run so that the cost of the last unit of investment is covered by the charge made to consumers. We have already seen in earlier chapters how intimately investment and pricing are linked, and this is especially true in the depletion decision. The basic problem is to distribute resources not only at any one moment of time but also through time so that the limited natural resources yield maximum benefit to the community. (In practice the market-surplus argument for marginal-cost pricing analyses only benefit to consumers and producers, but this is virtually the whole community for a universally used product like oil which is an input to so many productive processes. However, the distribution of the surplus within the community must be an important issue in Government policy.) The key to determining the optimum rate of depletion is in knowing what the alternatives for consumption will be when the current sources of oil are exhausted. These are likely to be employed in a number of stages rather than by one sudden change from North Sea oil to a single more expensive alternative. For example, even while there are still plenty of reserves, exploitation may gradually move to less geologically favourable, and more expensive, fields, though this will also be affected by the licensing system. Similarly when the exploitation of oil in the North Sea is no longer commercially viable, there may be temporary fuel sources available (perhaps substitute natural gas) before the oil is more permanently replaced by, say, nuclear energy. Because, eventually, some more expensive fuel may replace North Sea oil, an element of resource cost is involved in its use. In practice the resource costs of using a barrel of oil may be less important in setting its price to the consumer (which will normally be determined by world prices) than in ascertaining its value to the economy at various times, and hence the optimal rate of exploitation. Suppose that these real costs to the country of oil consumption are to be estimated. The resource costs of using a barrel of oil today include the discounted values of the costs of bringing forward by one barrel the times when each of these more expensive alternatives must be instituted. The nearer each of these steps comes, the higher is likely to be this resource-cost element. Perhaps the best way to show this is by a simple hypothetical example. Suppose that there are only two oil fields to be exploited consecutively, one expected to last ten years and the other twelve years, and that at the end of twenty-two years the cheapest alternative will be to buy oil from abroad (available in unlimited quantities) at three pence per unit. The costs of exploiting the two fields are supposed to be one and two pence per unit respectively. The resource cost (additional to resources used directly in exploitation) of using one unit of oil now from the cheaper field is that of having to use an extra unit from the more expensive field in ten years time and to buy another unit in twenty-two years time. The present value of this scarcity cost, discounted at 10 per cent (another arbitrary figure) is $(2 - 1)/(1 + 0 \cdot 1)^{10} + (3 - 2)/(1 + 0 \cdot 1)^{22}$, that is $0 \cdot 509$ pence per unit. However, the year before the first field runs dry, the discounted cost will be $(2 - 1)/(1 + 0 \cdot 1) + (3 - 2)/(1 + 0 \cdot 1)^{13}$ or $1 \cdot 199$ pence per unit. For intervening years the cost would be gradually increasing within this range. The forecasting problem is made more difficult, however, by the need to feed back into the 'model' the effect of this resource cost on the rate of exploitation. Perhaps the addition of this value would suggest a more conservative policy so that the life of each field would be extended by one year. The scarcity element now would fall to $(2 - 1)/(1 + 0 \cdot 1)^{11} + (3 - 2)/(1 + 0 \cdot 1)^{24}$ or $0 \cdot 452$ pence per unit. The effect of this new element on the value of the oil, and hence on depletion, must be re-examined to see that the model yields internally consistent results.

In practice the technique suggested here for basing oil-depletion policy on minimising net-present-value resource costs to the economy (equivalent to maximising net-present-value benefits) would involve a number of difficulties, mainly because of uncertainty in various factors. One of these is the rate of technical development which may keep the costs of exploitation constant over time (despite less favourable geological conditions as development proceeds) if present projects on semi-submersible rigs prove feasible. It is also very difficult to predict the exact geological characteristics of future discoveries and the cost of the fuels that may replace oil in various uses when there are no more recoverable North Sea deposits. In the face of these uncertainties it would probably be necessary to undertake the type of exercise suggested above with a variety of forecasts to examine the implications of each, and of errors in central estimates.

Perhaps the most controversial element in calculating resource costs is deciding on the rate of discount; in this case a rate of 10 per cent has been used, but it has been argued in Chapter 4 (and it is evident from current (1976) real rates of interest) that this rate is probably a considerable over-estimate of the real social time preference rate. Even 5 per cent may be on the high side, but it is a useful figure to provide a comparison of the effects of different rates of discount. Returning to the original assumptions of one pence per unit difference in costs for each of the fields and the bought-in oil and ten- and twelve-year lives for the fields, the resource-cost element with a 5 per cent discount rate would be $1/(1 + 0 \cdot 05)^{10} + 1/(1 + 0 \cdot 05)^{22}$, that is $0 \cdot 956$ pence per unit. Thus we have almost doubled the scarcity value by halving the discount rate. The discount rate used is likely to have a significant effect on the optimum solution, at least in the long run, and poses considerable problems for estimating the optimum resource cost, price levels and depletion rates. The principles of determining the discount rate have been discussed in Chapter 4, with no very satisfactory solution. It is important to realise that oil companies are likely to use significantly higher rates of discount than the Government, partly because of tax considerations and partly because they increase rates to reflect the risky nature of the investment. The implications of these discrepancies have been discussed in previous chapters; and they are likely to result in a divergence between optimum depletion policies as viewed by oil companies and Government, with the latter usually taking a more conservative view. (Indeed the present administration (1976) has felt it necessary to assure the oil companies that it will *not* impose restrictions on exploitation before 1982; until this date the interests of all parties to attain self-sufficiency in oil production as quickly as possible are likely to coincide.) The discount rate used can have significant effects on the optimum solution in the model, and considerable thought should therefore be given to its value.

The only obvious comment to make about the level of discount rate is that the usual rates (traditionally 8 to 10 per cent) are likely to be too high in real terms and so may result in considerable underestimates of the true scarcity value. This is especially true in cases where the S.T.P.R. rather than opportunity cost of capital for investment may be relevant because the main issue is the timing of consumption. This is clearly so in exploiting reserves, though it is an over-simplification to ignore altogether the private possibilities for investment. For example, some of the resources used in oil production might be released for use elsewhere in the economy if exploitation is delayed, just as some of the benefits which accrue may be in financial rather than consumption form and so become available for private investment. One development profile, for example, might involve rapid exploitation in the early years to yield financial gains from exports; these could then be re-invested to provide for consumption at a future date. Thus even if some benefits do accrue in financial terms, the main choice in exploitation is between consumption now and consumption later, so the appropriate discount rate is probably one weighted heavily in favour of the S.T.P.R. (It should be noted that the example used above for illustrative purposes has large jumps in costs of alternative sources of oil relative to the absolute cost of exploitation. Thus, although the doubling of the scarcity value by halving the discount rate may be a general result, the large proportionate effect which it has on costs may not be. It should be emphasised again that the figures chosen are purely arbitrary, and are selected chiefly for simplicity of exposition. The analysis has ignored any production constraints such as are likely to operate in exploiting the wells, to maintain pressure in the pipeline and to ensure 'good oil-field practice'.)

We have so far been concerned with problems in determining the resource costs of oil use, but there are difficulties, too, in allocating some of the private costs of exploitation. These arise from two main areas – the nature of oil and gas exploration, and the fact that crude oil is refined into a number of different fuels and oil products. Both these factors give rise to some difficulty in allocating costs. In any exploration for oil, some dry wells are almost inevitable in the search for fuel, and the cost of such unproductive work is part of the expense of oil recovery. It seems only logical to include some average number of dry wells as part of the cost of the productive drilling. The appropriate average may vary according to expectations of a commercial oil strike at each well; for example, it is likely to be different for an unexplored sector of the sea bed and one that is already known to be surrounded by oil-bearing rock. But some allowance for dry wells needs to be made in estimating exploitation costs in each case. There is also a 'joint-product' element in exploration, for in some cases drilling is undertaken to find both gas and oil, and these may be found together, or one fuel may be discovered when the other was being sought. This complicates slightly the estimate of an appropriate 'dry-well' ratio. For if a company seeking oil finds gas, this is theoretically a dry well with an *ex gratia* gas find. However, since it is probably impossible to ascertain reliably the anticipations of a drilling company, and the best guide to an appropriate dry-well ratio is past experience, this may be more a theoretical problem than a practical one. If gas and oil are found together, there may also be joint costs of a common platform, drilling facilities and pipeline to be allocated between the products if different marketing strategies, tax liabilities and cost-related prices are to be instituted. Here the problems of cost allocation may be quite significant and present real difficulties.

To allocate the joint costs of exploitation of a barrel of crude oil to the various products into which it is eventually refined also raises problems. The refinement process is so complex that a full analysis of it would require (and has resulted in) a number of full-length books, and the calculation of both private and social costs to the consumer presents considerable practical problems. For example, if the oil is exploited mainly to provide heavy-fuel oil, and light distillates are merely a 'by-product', it may not be appropriate to allocate the scarcity premium in the same proportion (by value) to the two products. Some adjustment of the refining process to vary the proportions of output is possible, but this is limited by technical considerations so that calculation of the allocation of private and resource costs may be difficult. (Again the example chosen is purely arbitrary – in practice, demand for both these particular oil products is likely to be high. The United Kingdom's own oil reserves seem to contain a high proportion of lighter fractions and to yield quite a large amount of the more expensive distillates. It may prove profitable to concentrate refining to produce as much as possible of these more valuable oil factors, and to exchange some of this output for cheaper imported heavy oils.)

So far the discussion of costs has concentrated on depletion policy and its relation to timing of demand rather than on the allocation of any surplus which arises from North Sea oil reserves. However, that such surplus exists is evident as another facet of the 'resource element' in costs. This surplus consists of the difference between the market price obtainable for the oil and the total costs of extracting and distributing it. Theoretically the existence of such surplus should attract more suppliers into the industry, expanding supply and so bringing down the price until all but 'normal profit' has been eliminated. This is unlikely to happen in the North Sea, however, because of the nature of the product and its supply. Only a limited number of companies possess the ability to raise finance and the necessary expertise to exploit the oil, and these are apportioned sectors of the North Sea by a licensing system. In any case the supply of oil is not very price-elastic in the short term, and in the long run the total supply is fixed so that the expansion of supplies may mean exploiting more expensive sources as the price rises. The world price of oil has been pushed up considerably in the early 1970s by political and economic moves in the Arab world, so that the price obtainable for North Sea fuel has also risen. Thus, for a number of reasons, there is a gap, or rent (though oil companies and government might argue about its magnitude) between revenue obtainable from, and total costs of, supplying oil from the continental shelf.

There has been considerable discussion on where and how this economic rent should be allocated, especially since the report of the Select Committee on Nationalised Industries on the subject in 1975 and the election of a Labour Government in February of the previous year. The licensing for oil exploration was an extension of the natural-gas licensing system, so that the Government had seen no need for more than a nominal licence fee in return for permission to exploit any oil in a particular area (these licences were granted according to the work programme laid down). This system is open to criticism even in the gas case, where some of the surplus should be liable to capture by the British Gas Corporation (see, for example, Dam [1970]); the Gas Corporation can buy gas from the exploiting oil companies at a price representing cost plus normal profit, and sell to the consumer at market-related prices. The difference between these prices (allowing for distribution costs) is the economic rent, which can then be returned to the Treasury and thence to the Government. However, in practice some of the surplus may be lost in maintaining the British Gas Corporation, and because of political pressure to keep prices down, some may also be used as subsidies to gas consumers. In the case of oil the problem is likely to be even greater. For here the oil companies have to incur only the costs of exploration and extraction but are able to sell the oil through private retail outlets at the market price, thus recouping most of the surplus in the form of profits. Some of this would be recovered through royalties paid to the Government by the oil companies (designed as a payment for the destruction of a natural resource) but these are not high enough to reduce profits to a 'normal' level at expected oil prices. The Government might remove some of the surplus by corporation tax on profits, but it seemed possible that this could be evaded by non-U.K. firms, and would in any case leave most of the surplus with the oil companies. It was to remedy this situation and to attempt to regain some of the surplus for the citizens of the United Kingdom that the Government introduced a petroleum revenue tax in early 1975. This was to be applied with corporation tax and royalties and was designed so that about 70 per cent of oil companies' profits (or economic rent) was paid to the Government, but with special allowances and safeguards to maintain exploitation incentives for marginal fields. Here some of the problems already mentioned of determining and defining private costs of exploration are relevant, since the oil companies and the Government, facing each other in a bargaining situation, are each likely to exaggerate their own interests. This makes it difficult to ascertain the most appropriate level of taxation which will ensure that the interests of the country are served by recouping most of the rent and exploiting all viable reserves while allocating a reasonable profit to the oil companies.

However, it may be less easy to control the *rate* of exploitation by the tax level; clearly the economic returns expected are likely to affect oil companies' decisions to some extent, but taxation may prove a clumsy instrument if used primarily for this purpose. Until self-sufficiency in oil production is attained (probably about 1980), the interests of the oil companies and the Government coincide in exploiting the reserves as rapidly as possible to achieve that position. After this date their estimates of the optimum rate of depletion may differ, and here the British National Oil Corporation, by direct involvement in the production and distribution of oil, should be able to represent the Government's interests in the depletion decision. Other things being equal, the oil companies would like to exploit their finds as rapidly as possible to cover the cost of their capital investment. If there is a possibility of oil prices increasing sharply in the future, they may prefer to keep back some of the oil to take advantage of the greater potential returns, but only if the net benefit to them of such a move at least covers the rate of interest they are paying on capital. However, we have already seen in Chapter 4 and elsewhere in this book that the rate of interest payable by private firms is not necessarily that at which consumption benefits to the country should be discounted, and indeed the former will usually be higher. Thus some restraint on exploitation may be necessary if the optimum rate from the country's rather than the oil companies' point of view is to be implemented.

One problem in determining how best to exploit the reserves of the North Sea is in considering how it will fit in with wider economic objectives and constraints. The existence of British oil has sometimes been hailed as the solution to all our ills, economic at least, and with this attitude there is usually associated an assumption that this panacea should be extracted as rapidly as possible. We have already seen that from the point of view of optimally allocating resources through time, a slower rate of depletion may be preferable; but there are other factors to consider since the fuel sector is so central to the rest of the economy and is one in which substantial Government economic planning already takes place. Because of this central and vital role the Government may wish to safeguard all fuel supplies so that if the United Kingdom becomes politically or economically isolated she has her own secure supply. The implications of maintaining this security may be equivalent to placing a premium on oil reserved for future home use rather than exported for present returns.

Whatever the rate of exploitation it is likely to lead to a reduction in the balance-of-payments deficit, though this may not be an even process, nor a wholly beneficial one. Initially improved balance of payments would enable a reduction of foreign debts and an increase in the standard of living, perhaps sufficient to establish self-sustained growth in the future. However, oil development itself involves the use of imported capital goods and services, so that the oil balance of payments may become negative again after self-sufficiency has been achieved because of the outflows from loan repayments and remittances abroad by foreign oil companies (Everingham *et al.* [1975]). Even ignoring this temporary setback, a generally improved balance of payments may lead to exchange appreciation and a loss of competitiveness for U.K. goods *vis-à-vis* foreign alternatives both at home and abroad. The demand for imports generated by the new 'oil-based' prosperity may well continue after the oil which originally financed it is exhausted. A rapid rate of depletion which provides sufficient supplies to export oil as well as meeting home needs is particularly open to this danger. Similarly in the balance-of-payments context as well as others some account must be taken of the rate at which the economy can adjust, both as the oil is first exploited and later when it is exhausted. Because the economy in practice does not consist of a set of instantaneously adjusting perfect markets these dynamic considerations are important. So, too, is the effect on other aspects of fuel policy. Chapter 13 shows how calculating the true cost of mining coal, and hence its appropriate market price, depends on the job prospects for miners and the total demand for coal, which is itself largely determined by markets for other fuels. Similarly resource allocation within the entire fuel sector must be considered in determining how best to exploit North Sea oil. The need for such an exercise arises from the divergence of private and social costs inherent in the difference between market rates of interest and the optimum rate of discount. Basically the issue is to determine the second-best position, but, as we have seen, this raises large and important issues of investment appraisal and allocation of market surplus. Like most economic problems it is far from easily resolved, and the uncertainties involved suggest it would be most sensibly and comprehensively approached using a sensitivity analysis to examine the implications of different rates of depletion. Indeed this issue raises clearly many of the principles of investment, pricing policies and reconciliation of different objectives suggested in earlier chapters. While this discussion has not attempted to define answers to these complex questions, it is hoped that it has provided a practical context to illustrate how the more abstract concepts should be brought into the decision-making process.

Suggestions for Further Reading

K. W. DAM, 'Oil and Gas Licensing in the North Sea', *Journal of Law and Economics*, vol. 7 (1964).

M. V. POSNER, *Fuel Policy: A Study in Applied Economics* (London: Macmillan, 1973).

SELECT COMMITTEE ON NATIONALISED INDUSTRIES, *Nationalised Industries and the Exploitation of North Sea Oil and Gas*, H.C.P. 345 (London: H.M.S.O., April 1975).

Chapter 11

Peak-Load Pricing

The issue of peak pricing is one which has often been raised as part of the marginal-cost-pricing controversy; it illustrates well some of the basic principles of price policy, as well as some pitfalls which exist in its application, and this chapter is in some ways an extension of the themes introduced in Chapter 7.

Peak-load pricing becomes feasible when demand varies with time and a common supply system is used at both peak and non-peak periods. The solution sought is one which reflects the costs at various times and simultaneously discourages consumers from overloading the system when it is already most intensively used; in fact the optimum solution satisfying each criterion is the same, as we shall see, but considerable confusion can arise if at the outset it appears that possibly incompatible solutions to two separate problems are being sought.

The first example of the peak/off-peak issue to be given prominence in the literature was that of the railways (Hotelling [1938]); like many other peak-load-pricing examples, railways have large and indivisible fixed costs, some of which (lines and signalling systems for example) are available for both peak and non-peak travel. The size of the total system is likely to be determined by the maximum demand it has to meet. However, this does not mean, as is often supposed, that investment in such equipment will only take place as a result of increases in peak demand. For an increase in demand at a time when the system is close to capacity may make it economic to change the structure of the system by incurring additional capital expenditure. For example, a level crossing which is frequently used at peak periods but little during the rest of the day may be intensively operated by hand during three hours a day but rarely at other times. However, an increase in non-peak rail traffic may make it impracticable for one man to manipulate the gates because he is required to be 'on call' almost continuously, and so such increased demand may require the installation of automatic barriers. In this case the changing pattern of demand caused by an increase in off-peak travel involves incurring capital expenditure to reach the new optimum pattern of supply. The case is even clearer for fuel industries, electricity for example, which meet peak demand by capital-cheap, expensive-to-run methods and have a range of generating plant extending to equipment used to meet base load which is usually expensive to install but has low operating costs. An increase in off-peak demand may in this case make it economic to install more low-running-cost plant which can then be used to supply both peak and off-peak demand. Thus capital expenditure may arise from an increase in non-peak demand even when there is some excess capacity. This point has been emphasised here as well as in earlier chapters because it is easy to assume that the difference between peak and non-peak marginal costs coincides with that between long-run and short-run costs. This misconception is understandable, for an increase in peak demand would involve expanding the system to meet it, thus incurring capital expenditure, while any non-peak increase in demand *could* be met by using spare capacity which existed to supply the peak. Although it is true that non-peak demand can be met in this way, we have seen that, by changing the optimum pattern of supply, changes in off-peak demand may incur capital expenditure.

The long-run/short-run distinction has been raised misleadingly as an aid in marginal-cost-pricing interpretation in various contexts, and appeared in another guise when the discovery of North Sea gas rendered much town gas equipment prematurely obsolete. Since there was unlikely to be new investment in such equipment, it appeared that the marginal costs of town gas supply were of a short-run nature. However, this is likely to confuse rather than clarify the issue, for there may well be parts of the town gas supply system which need to be renewed before the switch to natural gas is complete. The only 'fool-proof' way of determining any long-run marginal costs is to go back to the basic definition that it is the difference between total costs of the optimal system with an increment of demand, and the optimal system without the extra demand; as we have seen, the best supply pattern may vary even if total capacity remains the same. The only special consideration which applies to a system with variable demand is the classification of demand into peak and off-peak (which is not always a straightforward matter).

Another attempt to connect the peak pricing issue with familiar concepts has been made in identifying part of the returns from higher peak prices as an economic rent (Hotelling [1938]). It was argued that since some of the system was common to both peak and off-peak supply, any revenue which covered more than operating costs at each level of use was a form of rent. This often arose because the demand exceeded capacity if prices equalled operating costs, so the necessity to raise prices as a form of rationing was seen as a return to the 'scarcity' of capacity in the system. For example, in railway systems, operating costs might be considered to include the costs of manning signals and stations and running trains but not of providing and maintaining track. Any revenue over and above the operating costs would appear as a 'bonus' to the operating industry. The fallacy in this argument is to regard any of the system as fixed in this way, for it can nearly always be expanded in some way, if only at considerable expense (for example, it is estimated that Victoria Station in London cannot accommodate any more traffic at peak hours, so that increased demand could be met only by expanding another station or perhaps building a new terminus). However, these costs of expansion, however high, are the true peak marginal costs, and it is these that should be charged to peak units. Then, although there may be a period of adjustment while extra facilities are provided, marginal-cost pricing will ensure that the system can cope with all who are prepared to pay the marginal cost, so that no other system of rationing will be necessary. Of course, in practice, there may be exceptions to this neat solution if, for example, the Government considers that private costs exceed social costs and so wishes to charge less to consumers than the marginal cost of supply. This is implicit in their subsidy of British Rail's London commuter services where the peak charges are often less than off-peak prices (through season tickets and other concessions). If the Government is prepared to back its priorities, it should provide the difference between the revenue collected and that necessary to expand the system if peak demand exceeds capacity for supply; in practice, however, other economic and political priorities are likely to frustrate such an ideal. It should also be pointed out that there are cases where true economic rent arising from scarcity does arise – for example, in the case of natural resources such as gas and oil whose total quantity is fixed (see Chapter 10 for a discussion of some of the economic issues in this case). However, truly rigid supply rarely occurs in other circumstances, so that genuine marginal-cost pricing at each level of demand should ensure that the system is expanded to meet demand (though not necessarily that the enterprise as a whole covers cost, but only that marginal investment is recovered).

The exact definition of peak and off-peak demand, and the extent to which they should be further differentiated, may give rise to some practical problems. For example, in the case of electricity the marginal cost at any moment is the marginal cost of the 'marginal' generating station plus the costs of distribution at the particular loading of the system. These marginal costs may vary continuously, and in theory a marginal-cost tariff should reflect all levels within this range. In practice, however, there are two obstacles to such a course: the expense of implementing the tariff and the impracticability of ensuring that each consumer is constantly aware of exactly what costs his consumption incurs. This latter is the most serious problem, since the chief object of a marginal-cost tariff is to enable consumers to base decisions on the costs they incur, and if this message function cannot be maintained, its justification is undermined. There are also problems of forecasting the level of marginal costs, a difficulty in any pricing system which involves notifying consumers of tariffs in advance of consumption; it is likely to be particularly severe, however, if there are a large number of different tariff levels because the errors of forecasting may become a significant proportion of the difference between the various prices.

If continuous tariff variation to reflect marginal costs is not practicable, how many different tariffs should be applied? One extreme alternative would involve averaging marginal costs over all demand conditions (that is over all parts of the day and year) so that consumers faced only one tariff, and in some circumstances this might be the most appropriate solution. In between there are an infinite number of possibilities with tariffs differentiating to various extents between types of consumer and time of consumption. The optimum compromise is determined by the balance between the cost of imposing different tariffs and the responsiveness of demand to changes in price. Thus if demand is not responsive to price variations at different times, but only to the over-all cost of consumption, it is not so important to ensure that consumers face the correct marginal costs at each moment. However, there is a trap here which is easy to fall into when considering fuel tariffs. This is that although the consumer may use his appliance at a given intensity once he has bought it, regardless of changes in the cost of fuel (for example someone who has installed a central-heating system is likely to use it when it is cold even though fuel is more expensive then), if it is average costs of consumption over the year which determine appliance use, it is important that consumers realise that some appliances are more expensive to use on an annual basis because they use a higher proportion of peak fuel than others. Thus if the electricity industry were to determine that, once purchased, appliances are used at the same rate regardless of annual variations in cost of electricity, it might decide that an average marginal-cost tariff for power over the year would be adequate. But this would suggest to consumers that the cost of using electricity over the year is the same per unit for cooking or heating; in fact the average annual marginal cost is much higher for heating since in this use there is a lower load factor (ratio of average to maximum daily consumption) and therefore a higher proportion of expensive peak units for a given number of units used during the year. Thus although an average marginal-cost tariff may be adequate in some circumstances, the consumers must be shown that different tariffs are appropriate for different uses, particularly when they are deciding on appliance purchases. (In practice it is hard to imagine uses for which demand is totally price-inelastic, even given appliance installations. For example, in cooking, which might be considered one of the least price-sensitive uses of energy, economies may be possible by using the oven for several dishes simultaneously or by concentrating its use at the weekend if fuel is cheaper then. What may be true in many cases, however, is that the resource savings available from such economies do not justify incurring the costs of a highly differentiated system of tariffs.)

The cost of implementing differentiated tariffs is an important determinant of how far variations in cost of supply should be reflected by a proliferation of different prices. In general it is not worth further differentiating tariffs if the resources saved by the resulting reallocation of demand do not exceed those used in implementing the change. In the transport sector it is comparatively easy to charge different rates to passengers travelling at different times, and indeed this is a common practice in the railway industry. It should be remembered, however, that such variations in tariffs are only useful if the consumer is fully aware of them so that he bases his consumption decisions accordingly. This is one difficulty which arises in any complex system of fuel tariffs where costs vary considerably between peak and off-peak demand; a complicated tariff system reflecting these variations accurately may only confuse the consumer and so worsen, if anything, his allocation of demand (from the viewpoint of his own welfare). The cost of implementing peak and off-peak tariffs would be much less in the electricity than in the gas industry for the obvious reason that electric switches between meters can be used more easily in the former case; the costs of providing more than one meter per consumer in the gas industry and of registering consumption at different times on each might well be prohibitively expensive compared with the benefits achieved. The coal and oil industries, which also experience seasonal demand, can vary prices in winter to reflect the additional costs of storage incurred and so 'encourage' consumers to buy in the summer and incur storage costs themselves. It is the constraints implied by the nature of the industry, and the responsiveness of demand to different seasonal and daily tariffs, which determine how far peak-load tariffs should be implemented.

Perhaps the clearest way of illustrating some of the issues involved is to consider one particular industry, gas, which experiences wide variations in cost from season to season but where the cost of complex metering is high. Ideally the tariff would charge according to each cost determinant, but such a procedure is not practical in every case. For example, the charges related to peak would require a method of measuring peak consumption separately from non-peak consumption in the same metering period, and of letting the consumer know that his consumption at that time was being charged at peak rates. A specific peak metering system does seem impracticable, but an alternative is to charge for gas consumed in different metering periods at different rates, according to average costs incurred by consumption in each period; a charge for peak can be included with the commodity charge for the period in which the peak falls by calculating the likely load factor for each consumer during that period. This does not give the consumer a specific message about peak use as such, but provides a general indication of total costs incurred according to his level of consumption during the peak period. If consumption over the period which includes peak is known, peak consumption can be estimated from knowledge of the gas appliances used.

To estimate peak consumption from over-all consumption in a period, several assumptions must be made about the load factors involved in heating and other gas appliances. Physical laws determine that the loss of heat between one closed space and another is proportional to the temperature difference between them. Thus if gas is used to heat a closed space to a certain temperature, the heat needed is proportional to the difference between the temperature in the space and that outside. (This proportionality breaks down if the space is not self-contained, for example if a window is open, but as no general extension of the principle is possible in such circumstances this possibility is ignored for the present approximations.) If gas appliances are the sole means of heating a space such as a room or a house, to a given temperature the ratio of maximum gas usage to average usage is the same as the ratio of maximum temperature difference to average temperature difference, and so peak consumption can be calculated if the average is known. In practice it is the average of temperatures below that at which the consumer keeps his house which is relevant, since it is only when the temperature falls below this level that he uses fuel for heating. A problem arises if gas appliances are not the sole means of heating, that is if electricity or coal or oil is used to supplement gas heating; in this case the ratio of maximum to average usage will apply to all the heat used, but not to gas consumption by itself. Consider two examples, gas central heating with an electric fire to provide extra heat, and, second, electric storage radiators for background heat with a gas fire for boosting the temperature when the weather is especially cold. In the first case gas provides a smaller proportion of total heat generated when the temperature is low and the electric fire is used most intensively; this means that a calculation based on gas heating alone will over-estimate gas supplied at peak as a proportion of average gas consumption. In the second situation the storage heaters provide most of the heat during fairly cold weather, but the gas fire is used much more in very cold weather, especially where this is unexpected and the storage heaters have not been adjusted to allow for it; in this case the peak consumption of gas will be under-estimated as a proportion of average consumption over the time period concerned. If a marginal-cost-pricing system were instituted by both the gas and electricity industries, and both used appliance ownership to estimate peak consumption, enough information might be available to allow for such discrepancies. However, appliance ownership is not equivalent to usage, and in any case this would not solve the problem of the consumer using coal or oil to supplement gas heating appliances. For the sake of simplicity, however, it is assumed that peak consumption and average consumption for heating appliances are in the same proportion as peak and average temperature differences, since there is insufficient information on equipment to examine the alternatives in any detail. How important discrepancies in charges would be depends on how they would affect the two consumer decisions — appliance investment and appliance use. In giving guidance for appliance investment it is the relative average cost of use of the various fuels which is important, and the assumption that only gas, say, is being used seems an adequate price guide to the consumer. In using appliances, however, consumers need more accurate information on the costs incurred in using various fuels. For example, it is sensible to encourage the use of electric heating during the winter plateau, but to use gas for extra peak heating, as it is peak electricity consumption which is very expensive (since it cannot be stored) and costs of winter gas supply depend more on the total quantity supplied during winter plateau demand. The importance of errors in calculating the proportion of gas in winter used at peak thus depends on the difference in peak and non-peak costs and on how sensitive demand is to differentials between peak and non-peak tariffs. This last factor is one which can only be determined by pilot experiments with different forms of tariff.

The choice of what time to choose as the 'winter period', during which a peak charge is incorporated, still remains. This must be the same length for each householder since otherwise it might be considered unfair, and it should if possible contain the 'peak day'. Usually peak consumption is in January or February, but it has occasionally fallen outside that period. A specific three-month period means that all meters must be read on the first and last days, and this would clearly increase the cost of reading considerably; one compromise would be to allow the winter quarter to extend a week in either direction; even then it would not invariably include the peak and makes the possibility of a four-month winter period attractive.

Fortunately the costs if the peak falls outside the winter quarter are not particularly serious for gas; for the main seasonal cost element is determined by the total quantity of gas used in the winter period when demand is greater than direct supply from the North Sea, and storage or additional production costs must be incurred. Indeed a six-month winter metering period in which the tariff reflects the costs of providing storage capacity might be more appropriate than a specific peak charge. As most costs are related to total winter demand, the consequences of the peak falling outside the 'winter quarter' would not be serious since the general message that winter use of gas is more expensive than summer use will already have been taken into account in appliance-purchasing decisions. It seems unlikely that consumers are very sensitive to variations in cost once they have bought appliances, and unlikely that they would shift demand substantially to a time when the winter tariff was not in force.

The choice of the winter 'peak' metering period must be a balance of two considerations: to include the peak as often as possible and yet to keep the period sufficiently short to give consumers a meaningful message about different costs at various times of the year. If the cost of meter-reading and billing were negligible, and if the timing of peak demand could be forecast and peak charges notified to consumers, the week of peak consumption could be metered and charged for separately to give the most accurate cost messages to consumers. Forecasts of peak demand are made easier by a slight lag in the reaction of gas demand to temperature changes, and by improved weather-forecasting techniques. Nevertheless it would be difficult to know of heavy demand more than a week or so in advance and there would be no guarantee that even greater demand would not follow later in the winter; and in practice meter-reading and billing are expensive, so some compromise between the accuracy of consumer messages and the cost of providing them must be found. One solution, if it is not feasible or desirable to read all meters in a small time period (for example a fortnight, as suggested above), is to charge consumers according to the proportion of their metering period which falls within the 'peak period'. Thus all consumers would pay a total of, say, three months' consumption at the peak-inclusive rate, but might have this spread over two bills.

An example of how the tariff could operate may illustrate these concepts. Suppose that a consumer uses gas for central heating and cooking, and one-twentieth of the gas consumed in the winter quarter is for cooking. If the average consumption of gas is x therms per day, then $19x/20$ is for heating, which has a winter-load factor of about $2/3$ (derived from assumptions outlined above) and $1/20 . x$ is used in cooking which we can assume to have unit load factor. Maximum daily consumption is

$$\left[\left(\frac{3}{2} \times \frac{19x}{20} \right) + \frac{1x}{20} \right] = \frac{59x}{40}.$$

Using this method and estimates of gas used by different appliances and the number of appliances in each household, peak demand could than be calculated from average winter consumption.

This system would of course involve detailed knowledge of consumers' appliances, but this might not be difficult to maintain using as a basis the records obtained when the conversion from town to natural gas was implemented (see P.I.B., *Gas Prices* [1969]). More difficult to judge is just what the effect of changes in tariffs would be on demand; the electricity industry was caught unawares in this respect in implementing their off-peak tariffs, when a new peak in the afternoon was stimulated by consumers taking advantage of the cheaper rates at this time. Indeed the whole circuit of forecasting – marginal costs, prices, demand and hence costs – is likely to be one of the greatest problems in implementing a peak-load tariff system. The best solution is a sensitivity analysis to consider as accurately as possible the costs and benefits of the various alternatives for each industry. What is clear is that, however theoretically justified marginal-cost pricing may be, problems of variations in costs and forecasting uncertainties make it virtually impossible to introduce a tariff accurately reflecting these costs at all times. As in most economic problems the best compromise must be sought in each industry.

Suggestions for Further Reading

HAROLD HOTELLING, 'The General Welfare in Relation to Problems of Taxation and of Railway and Utility Rates', *Econometrica,* vol. 6 (1938).

H. S. HOUTHAKKER, 'Electricity Tariffs in Theory and Practice', *Economic Journal,* vol. 61 (1951).

J. R. NELSON (ED.), *Marginal Cost Pricing in Practice* (Englewood Cliffs, N.J.: Prentice-Hall, 1964).

RALPH TURVEY, *Optimal Pricing and Investment in Electricity Supply* (London: Allen & Unwin, 1968).

O. E. WILLIAMSON, 'Peak-load Pricing and Optimal Capacity under Indivisibility Constraints', *American Economic Review,* vol. 56 (1966).

Chapter 12

The Third London Airport – A Cost–Benefit Analysis

In 1968 the Government set up a Commission, chaired by Mr Justice Roskill, to consider the best site for a third London airport. This followed several years of speculation on where such a project should and would be placed and a vigorous campaign from those affected by Stansted Airport to prevent its development as a major civil airport. The Commission was thus dealing with issues which raised strong feelings in those living near potential sites, and it had the unenviable task of balancing and assessing these reactions to determine the optimal solution. In the context of these problems it turned to cost–benefit analysis for guidance, and this chapter uses the report as an example of how such an approach has been applied. The Commission was not unanimous in its recommendations, and as well as considering the majority line of argument and conclusions we shall also discuss Professor Buchanan's minority report and his reasons for disagreeing with his colleagues. The problem of the third London airport raises interesting issues for the wider field of cost–benefit analysis, so we shall look in some detail at the assessment of noise (especially in its effect on residents), time savings and air safety. First, though, let us consider the wider issues by following the Commission's own line of procedure.

The Commission was anxious not to omit from consideration any feasible site within reasonable distance of London, so drew up an extensive 'long list' of seventy-eight sites. From these a medium list of twenty-nine sites was compiled by assessing each site in terms of surface access, defence considerations and noise nuisance. These twenty-nine were then further reduced by two stages to four sites on which more detailed analysis was undertaken to determine the most suitable for a new airport. These four were chosen partly to give a representative selection of different types of site, as well as for their promise in their own right. They were Cublington in Buckinghamshire, Thurleigh in Bedfordshire, Nuthampstead in Hertfordshire and an offshore site at Foulness in Essex. A brief look at how these sites compared at this preliminary stage may give some feeling for the nature of the assessment that was needed. Foulness ranked most favourably on noise, defence and air-traffic-control considerations but carried a high penalty in terms of surface access and construction costs. Nuthampstead was the cheapest site to prepare and was also better than Cublington and Thurleigh for noise nuisance and air-traffic control. Cublington had cheapest surface-access costs, and Thurleigh gained on defence grounds. Thus the problem the Commission faced in assessing the sites was to compare the different advantages of each and determine which would yield the required facilities of an airport at least cost to the community as a whole.

The Commission sought to make its proceedings as public as possible and to invite opinion from all interested parties. These included experts on noise and defence aspects, the airlines, local authorities and local residents' pressure groups. Much of this evidence was referred to in the report and had clearly influenced the Commission's conclusions. These were largely based on a cost–benefit analysis conducted by its own research team, though the C.B.A. results were not viewed uncritically, or accepted without some further discussion. Indeed the analysis was revised at one stage to include some further considerations and techniques. However, it is the general approach of the study which interests us here.

In estimating costs and benefits, products which commanded a market price were valued at resource costs, that is the market price net of taxes, subsidies and other transfers. There does not seem to have been any adjustment for imperfections within markets and their effect on prices, except so far as these were due to transfers (in fact transfers may be used to bring the market price closer to some hypothetical 'true cost', for example in subsidising railway fares in rural areas, so the effect of considering costs and benefits net of such transfers may involve a move away from true resource costs). However, it will in practice make little difference whether taxes and subsidies are included in estimating costs, since as transfers between consumers and Government they will not affect the aggregate valuation of net benefit to society as a whole. Which price is used in the calculations is important only in so far as the most appropriate figure (namely that faced by consumers) is used in forecasting demand, and hence future market adjustments.

The approach taken by the research team can probably be most easily appreciated by reproducing its own summary of best estimates of costs and benefits (Table 4). This was a central estimate and several

TABLE 4

Commission on the third London airport (summary of best estimates of costs and benefits, £m. 1968 prices, discounted to 1975)

	Cublington	Foulness	Nuthampstead	Thurleigh
Third London airport construction	184·0	179·0	178·0	166·0
Extension/closure of Luton Airport	−1·3	10·0	−1·3	−1·3
Airport services	74·6	62·9	70·7	67·2
Meteorology	5·0	1·6	3·0	2·0
Airspace movement	960·0	973·0	987·0	972·0
Passenger user costs	887·0	1041·0	868·0	889·0
Freight user costs	13·4	23·1	17·0	13·9
Road capital	7·4	7·4	7·5	2·7
Rail capital	4·4	16·0	8·0	3·8
Air safety	0·5	2·5	0·5	0·5
Defence	66·0	20·0	52·0	73·0
Public scientific establishments	2·0	3·4	11·2	16·6
Private airfields	8·7	3·1	9·8	12·2
Residential conditions (noise, off-site)	9·0	3·6	19·0	5·6
Residential conditions (on site)	4·8	0	3·0	2·4
Luton noise costs	0	6·7	0	0
Schools, hospitals and public authority buildings (including noise)	2·5	0·8	4·1	4·9
Agriculture	3·1	4·2	7·2	4·6
Commerce and industry (including noise)	0·6	0·1	1·2	2·0
Recreation (including noise)	6·7	0·3	3·6	3·8
Work and service journeys to airport	26·2	26·5	24·4	25·4
TOTAL NET COSTS (DISCOUNTED TO 1975)	2264·6	2385·2	2273·9	2266·3
TOTAL NET COSTS EXPRESSED AS DIFFERENCE FROM LOWEST COST SITE	0	120·6	9·3	1·7

TABLE 5

Commission on the third London airport (inter-site differences with different assumptions, £m. 1968 prices discounted to 1975)

	Cublington	Foulness	Nuthampstead	Thurleigh
Cost–benefit study (Table 4)	0	121	9	2
Excluding foreign leisure	6	113	20	0
Leisure time zero	0	44	19	2
Leisure time doubled	0	197	0	1
Business time −25%	1	110	9	0
Business time +25%	0	131	10	3
N.N.I.* +5	0	120	17	0
No generated trips	8	84	0	7
No foreign leisure, N.N.I. +5	7	112	29	0
Business time −25% } Leisure time zero	10	42	28	0
Business time +25% } Leisure time zero	0	54	19	3
Business time + 25% } Leisure time doubled	0	208	1	3
Business time −25% } Leisure time doubled	9	195	8	0
Business time −25% } Leisure time zero } N.N.I. +5	11	43	37	0
Business time +25% } Leisure time zero } N.N.I. +5	0	54	27	2
Business time −25% } Leisure time doubled } N.N.I. +5	10	196	17	0
Business time +25% } Leisure time doubled } N.N.I. +5	0	208	9	2
No generated trips } Business time −25%	7	74	0	6
No generated trips } Business time +25%	7	94	0	8
No generated trips } Business time −25% } N.N.I. +5	5	67	4	0
No generated trips } Business time +25% } N.N.I. +5	1	85	2	0
No generated trips } N.N.I. +5	5	76	3	0

* Noise and Number Index: the measure of noise nuisance used in the United Kingdom.

sensitivity analyses were also conducted (assuming, for example, the value of leisure time to be zero, or double the central estimate, and the noise index to be increased in value). Table 5, showing the inter-site differences under these various different assumptions, is also reproduced as an example of how a sensitivity analysis can be used in such a study. Of course it is impossible to explain adequately the meaning and implication of each item in a brief survey of this kind, but it is hoped these two tables will give the reader some feel for the kind of approach used. (Considerable detail on the methodology and procedure is given in the seventh volume of the *Papers and Proceedings* of the Commission's report.)

The first issue to be determined in the C.B.A. was which rate of discount to use in converting the figures to present-value terms. Unfortunately this was not a factor on which a sensitivity analysis was conducted so it is difficult to estimate the effect of using a rate other than the 8 per cent figure the research team employed. This was chosen as the best representative of the average pre-tax return on risk-free investments in the private sector. Thus the research team were attempting to allow for some of the market distortions (by considering pre-tax returns) though of course this rate does not necessarily reflect a free-market equilibrium, as Chapter 4 has shown. Some length of life had to be assumed for the airport, and this was a difficult choice since the physical assets were likely to last almost indefinitely with suitable maintenance. The economic life therefore depended on the rate of technological change and when the airport's capacity would become obsolete, and on this basis a lifetime of thirty years was chosen. In practice, since each of the sites had some element of costs throughout its life which were greater than corresponding items at the alternative sites, the comparison rested mainly on these, and the relative attractiveness of each candidate would probably remain unaltered by assumptions about the length of life. However, a short life (and a high discount rate) would tend to penalise the airport with the heaviest construction costs (in this comparison, Foulness) since these costs then become relatively greater. However, although no sensitivity analysis was performed on this aspect, it does not seem that the length of life would have been a crucial factor. The research team itself pointed out that costs and benefits have already been heavily discounted at twenty-years' distance, for which the discount factor at 8 per cent per annum is 0·215. The base year was chosen as 1975, but the Commission recognised that the choice of the year in whose values the costs and benefits were expressed had no effect on the relative figures, but only on their magnitude.

Apart from the general problems (such as choosing a rate of discount) which afflict any cost–benefit analysis the Commission faced a number of specific problems typical of transport studies. One of these was how best to evaluate time savings to travellers, both in reaching the airport and in the length of air journeys. A distinction was made between working and leisure time, and although it was acknowledged that in some instances the division might not be clear-cut, in most cases this separation was feasible; the cost of working time was assumed to be at least the gross pay of the traveller, since this was presumably his marginal worth to his employer (though this assumption is challenged in the discussion of miners' marginal productivity in Chapter 13), or, if self-employed, the marginal opportunity cost of his own time. The suggestion that there were potential benefits from travelling time which could be spent on some form of work, or in leisure such as reading, and that these should be offset against the cost of time spent travelling, was dismissed because of the limited nature of the types of work or leisure feasible under these circumstances. Ignoring such opportunities for using travel time may lead to inaccuracy, since if a train or air journey is anticipated, appropriate reading can often be saved for the occasion, freeing the worker for other duties in the meantime. Indeed it is conceivable that given a choice between different forms of travel time a traveller might well be prepared to lengthen the total time spent travelling to achieve a relatively greater part which he could usefully employ in such activities (for example he may choose to travel by train rather than car, even if the latter is faster and the travel costs identical, if the train is likely to offer facilities for work unsuitable in a car). However, the Commission decided to ignore any such possible benefits; they would certainly be difficult to assess but their omission would be likely to penalise the assessment of the airport furthest from the centre of London, since journeys to and from it might contain a higher proportion of useful time than those to closer sites.

Ignoring any possible fruitful use of travelling time, the research team valued business hours at the full cost to the employer of the traveller's employment, that is his gross salary plus overheads. This was the basis on which the Ministry of Transport usually assessed working time, using average wages and salaries over the whole population for general purposes since these represent adequately the income of road and rail users. The average salary of air travellers, however, is likely to be higher than that for the whole population, so surveys of passengers at Heathrow and Gatwick Airports were conducted to obtain an appropriate figure for the travellers concerned.

The valuation of leisure time was much more controversial than that of business time. Again the Ministry of Transport's criterion was used and leisure time valued at one-quarter of (air travellers') gross income. These values have been imputed by observing how consumers behave when they have a choice between a fast, expensive journey and a slower but cheaper one. (One allowance must be made for the fact that travellers may not always be aware of the true cost of all the alternatives, for example many people under-estimate the total cost of car journeys.) The research team cites the example of travellers who have the choice between a quick journey over a river by toll bridge or a longer route over a free bridge. Careful cataloguing of route origins and destinations can help in estimating a valuation of travellers' time. Of course there are considerable individual variations in such values, but some average can be extracted. Since any consumer's value of products depends on his total income, the worth of travelling time, too, is assumed to be related to gross salary. In using the same proportion of income for air travellers' time as for the general population, the research team assumed that the fraction is invariant with income. This is not obviously so, and it might well be that as a consumer's income increases, so will his valuation of non-working travelling time as a proportion of his gross salary. This argument is suggested by considering leisure as a non-essential good which is consumed in a greater proportion to total expenditure as 'primary wants' are satisfied. This suggests that even if it can be reliably shown that the 'average' man values leisure time at a quarter of his income, a larger fraction may be suitable for air travellers – whose incomes are above average.

In its final hearings the Commission was faced with many criticisms of its time valuations. Most critics thought that the research team's valuations were too high, though some authorities agreed with its assessment. The Commission suggested that high and low values of business and leisure time above and below the original estimates should be used where appropriate, though the original values were used where a single figure was required.

A particular issue raised in the hearings was that the value of small time savings (say ten to fifteen minutes per journey) may be negligible. This was important because the difference in the journey time from central London to each of the four sites was between five and fifteen minutes. That such differences are irrelevant may seem intuitively attractive, and it is worth considering some of the reasons for which this

view was rejected. Although it is true, of course, that twelve savings of
five minutes are of a different nature than one of an hour, the research
team emphasised that it is not the time savings themselves but the use
which can be made of them which is important. Thus five minutes
saved from a journey, when added to other time available, may enable
a particular job to be undertaken for which there would otherwise be
insufficient time. The Commission also pointed out that all journeys
were not through central London and that time savings on these non-
metropolitan routes are also relevant. It suggested that to introduce
some cut-off point below which valuation of time is zero would be artificial, and, though this may be appropriate for some travellers, is unlikely to be a representative average. Indeed it is easy to sympathise
with a view which considers that time is not valued proportionately,
that is a single time saving may not always be worth twice a saving
half as long. There certainly seems no obvious reason why such a
linear relation should exist. However, in a cost–benefit analysis where
the average valuation of savings for many travellers is considered, any
such individual anomalies are likely to be absorbed by the aggregate
and so become insignificant. In any case such problems are unlikely to
be important in a comparison such as this where similar projects and
small time differences are under review. They might be more significant in a build/not-build project decision (for example the Fleet underground line or Channel Tunnel project) where the total value of
time must be compared with other costs and benefits, rather than in
this case where it is marginal differences between sites which are
important.

Another controversial issue which the research team and the Commission had to evaluate was that of noise nuisance. An airport at any
of the sites would obviously have unpleasant effects on the surrounding area because of the noise of aircraft, and the effect of this factor
on various categories of the population had to be assessed. As Table 4
shows, six categories of the population affected by noise were devised.
When the effects directly attributable to noise were extracted from
these items, the total costs incurred at each site amounted to £11
million for Foulness, £14 million (each) for Cublington and Thurleigh
and £24 million for Nuthampstead. The differences are clearly substantial and their assessment might certainly be significant in the choice
between Nuthampstead and either Cublington or Thurleigh. Like value
of travellers' time, the cost of noise nuisance is difficult to measure, and
therefore becomes controversial in the decision-making context. Noise

affected a wide variety of social activities and presented assessment problems in each case; these can be illustrated by sketching briefly the method used by the research team for estimating the noise nuisance to residences off the site of the airfield (those on-site would be compulsorily purchased and alternative accommodation provided for the occupants).

The first stage in assessing the effect of noise was to find some suitable general measure of noise nuisance at airports. Various suggestions were explored, including those used in air-traffic planning in France, West Germany and the United States. The measure chosen is known as the Noise and Number Index (N.N.I.) and has been widely used within the United Kingdom. It is composed of elements which represent both the average peak noise of aircraft and the frequency of flights, and was originally developed from a survey of residents near Heathrow Airport; each member of the sample was asked how far he felt affected by aircraft noise and the N.N.I. formula was developed to reflect these subjective reactions as closely as possible.

Having defined the measure of noise, N.N.I. contours could be calculated for each site operating at a particular capacity, and the area affected by noise can be estimated. Forecasting these contours depends on two factors – the frequency of aircraft movement and the noisiness of aircraft in the future. Both are difficult to assess, but particularly the latter, since by the year 2006 (that for which noise levels were estimated) the aircraft now operating are likely to have been replaced by a new generation of much larger jets. It seems highly likely that technology will have provided some solutions to the noise problem so that these new jets need be no more noisy than the smaller aircraft at present operating, and they could be much quieter. What is not easy to predict is the extent to which public opinion and noise-abatement regulations will have obliged operators to adopt these quieter but more expensive techniques. The Commission had to collate views and forecasts on this aspect and reach its own best estimate of traffic movements and noise in establishing the noise contours for each site. Any errors in this factor are likely to be less vital in a comparison of this kind where all four sites will be affected similarly than in a case where an airport is being compared with a project which creates no noise nuisance. However, to the extent that some sites are more seriously affected by noise (as clearly they are), any error in estimates would be reflected in relative costs.

Having established the effect of an airport in terms of N.N.I. contours, it remained to convert this effect to a monetary cost. The minimum noise level considered for residential-housing assessment was that deemed to cause 'a little annoyance' to the average resident. (Of course individual sensitivity to aircraft noise varies considerably, but the relevant figure in this context is the average for households affected.) The research team based its assessment of noise nuisance on the choice which off-site residents faced when this problem was introduced, namely to accept the noise nuisance, or to avoid it by moving and so losing the consumers' surplus enjoyed in their house (that is the difference between their valuation of it and the market price), the depreciation in value caused by the airport and the inconvenience and cost of moving. A rational consumer will choose whichever course yields him greater utility. The task of the research team was to measure the average value of the noise nuisance by assessing the various factors which would affect the householder's decision to move.

The consumers' surplus experienced by owner-occupiers was estimated by asking residents in areas similar to those around the four sites the price they would be prepared to accept for their houses; the amount by which this exceeded the market price represented their consumers' surplus plus the inconvenience and expense of moving. Some householders said they would not sell at any price and a few gave figures which implied a consumers' surplus greater than £5000, and in order not to distort the average the distribution of values of consumers' surplus was curtailed at this figure. Because the value of a particular house is likely to depend on how long the residents have been in the area and the network of social relations they have established, consumers' surplus was assumed to increase by 3 per cent per annum.

Depreciation of house values was assessed by a survey of the effect of Gatwick Airport on the surrounding residential area, which is similar to those around the proposed sites. Heathrow, in an area of much denser housing, was thought inappropriate as a guide in this case. As might be expected the survey showed that high-priced property depreciated by a larger proportion of its value than did lower-cost housing, and around Gatwick the depreciation figures ranged from 4·5 per cent to 29 per cent of property values. These estimates were used in the assessment of potential depreciation around each of the proposed sites.

An additional allowance for noise effects had to be made for Foulness because it was anticipated that Luton Airport would continue and expand its operations only if the Essex site was chosen. This would clearly cause additional inconvenience to Luton residents which would be avoided if the new airport was sited inland.

The total costs of noise nuisance to residents near each site was estimated by classifying the results into four categories of householders. One was those who moved out of the area because the noise nuisance from the airport exceeded the loss of consumers' surplus, removal and realisation of depreciation costs; their loss is the sum of these costs of moving. A second group of residents might be moving for other reasons, and the noise cost to them would be the depreciation on their houses, since the loss of consumers' surplus and removal expenses would have been incurred anyway; some householders would remain in the area, and for them the noise cost was derived by using a noise annoyance distribution and data from the depreciation of housing around Gatwick. A final category of householders affected by the new airport would be those moving into the area; for these there was no disbenefit from the airport since the decision to move into the locality implies that the noise nuisance is balanced by the cheaper purchase price of houses. From this model of the effects on different households, the total value of noise nuisance was estimated for owner-occupiers. The report makes no mention of a similar exercise for householders who rented their property in the affected areas. Although they would not suffer depreciation of the value of their property, they might similarly enjoy a consumers' surplus through long residence in the area, and would incur costs and inconvenience of removal if they wished to avoid the noise. In principle these could be included on the same basis as the estimates for those who owned their residences.

A third factor to be quantified which presented some difficulty was the difference in safety of operation at each of the sites. Because of the similarity of terrain and environment at each of the inland sites, there was thought to be no significant difference between them in this respect, but there were differences between the probability of the type of accidents and their consequences at the inland sites and at Foulness. These arose partly because the different surroundings made a sea rescue more likely at Foulness, but hazard to civilians outside the airport greater at the inland sites; and partly because the larger population of birds at Foulness incurred both greater control costs and greater hazards to aircraft.

The estimation of sea-rescue costs was straightforward. Statistics from airports in different types of terrain showed a slightly higher proportion of fatalities in water accidents, but the difference was not significant and the consequences of accidents for crew and passengers was assumed to be the same at each of the four sites. However, because swift rescue is vital for those not killed on impact, facilities would need to be provided at Foulness to reach and aid an aircraft which might come down in the water. This would probably be achieved by providing two hovercraft, and the cost of this provision was added to the Foulness 'account'.

Birds on airport sites cause costs both by increasing the chance of an accident caused by an aircraft striking a bird, and by necessitating a bird-control programme to reduce these risks. Because of its greater bird population, Foulness would require a larger and more expensive bird-scaring system than the other sites, which added to its relative costs. Even with appropriate bird-control programmes at each airport, the chance of bird strike is considerably greater at Foulness than at any of the inland sites. The cost of this increased risk was assessed by using past data on the number of bird-strike incidents at coastal and inland airports and the cost of aircraft damage which resulted. (Such an incident was not expected to cause injury or death.) These considerations all implied cost disadvantages for Foulness.

The other facet of safety costs was the probability of third-party injury, that is injury to those other than crew and passengers on the aircraft resulting from an accident. Here the inland sites were more expensive, for the area around Foulness was sparsely populated, and with flight paths largely over water the chances of injury to third parties was judged to be negligible. For inland sites data on third-party damage from jet accidents at other similar airports was used. This would probably over-estimate the probability of such injury since most airports are situated in more densely populated areas than the sites being considered. Indeed one accident where an aircraft had crashed into a housing estate very close to the runway killing seventy of the residents was excluded from the statistics because it was not thought representative of conditions at any of the inland sites. Past data suggested that in thirty years one accident involving third-party injury might be expected, and the average effect of such an accident would be four fatalities and four injuries. The 'timing' of such an event had to be related to the probability of its occurrence in relation to the number of aircraft movements in each year, and discounted accordingly. The costs of these fatalities and injuries were assumed to be the same as those used by the Ministry of Transport in road-casualty figures (based on life-insurance data), namely £9300 for each fatality and £625 for each casualty. There was no need to assess the costs of air-passenger deaths and injuries since the probability and severity of an accident at each of the sites was assumed to be equal, and so this factor would not affect the comparison between sites. If it did have to be evaluated, however, the Ministry of Transport figures might have to be revised if it was thought that air-crew and passengers' lives and injuries should be assessed differently from those of road-traffic-accident victims. The problems of evaluating damage to life and limb have been discussed in Chapter 8 and raise moral as well as economic issues. In this case it is interesting to note from Table 4 that the increased costs of search and rescue and those associated with the higher bird population at Foulness far outweighed the greater third-party hazard at the inland sites.

Of course the research team and the Commission were involved in assessing many other effects of using each of the sites for the third London airport (several were the subject of deep feeling and impassioned argument) and in evaluating the net effects. Care was taken to see that different relative values for costs and benefits should be considered, and, after hearing a great deal of evidence and considering the research team's report, the Commission decided that on balance Cublington had the net advantage. However, Professor Colin Buchanan submitted a minority report in which he expressed disagreement with the majority view and recommended that the airport be sited at Foulness. His obvious involvement with the choice and warmly argued note forms an odd contrast with the dispassionate tone of the rest of the report, and it is interesting to consider his reasons for disagreeing with the other eight members of the Commission. His arguments were based mainly on the contention that insufficient weight had been given to the various non-economic aspects of the decision, particularly to the loss of environment involved in any of the inland sites. He felt intuitively (as did many others) that despite its economic disadvantages the choice of Foulness was justified on these other grounds. In his note he pinpointed the basic dilemma of cost–benefit analysis, that valuations of non-monetary costs and benefits can never be unanimous. However, Table 4 shows that Foulness has a substantial cost disadvantage to overcome, so that its choice implies that the advantages it does possess are to be highly valued, and that the research team's efforts to evaluate them resulted in a gross under-estimate. It is difficult for any individual to achieve a satisfactory answer to these problems – introspection may suggest one result, a study of general views another, an implied figure from surveying behaviour on a revealed-preference basis yet another, while those who are thought to have 'enlightened' views in the area may suggest a fourth result. In the event the Government accepted the minority rather than the majority recommendation (perhaps because it valued political pressure more highly than had the Commission, or perhaps for the same reasons as Professor Buchanan gave) and announced that the third airport should be built at Foulness. However, it seems unlikely in 1976 that its decision will be implemented in the immediate future, and certainly not to start operations in 1980 as the Commission (including Professor Buchanan) had recommended. Indeed many have suggested that the whole Roskill Commission was a waste of money (the total cost was estimated at over a million pounds). Students of welfare economics can regard it as at least a useful exercise, despite its cost – like the subjects of cost–benefit analysis the exercises themselves yield benefits (in clarifying alternatives and building up a body of knowledge) which are difficult to evaluate in monetary terms; the use of this type of approach is surely preferable to unsubstantiated political arguments between different pressure groups which typically generate more heat than light.

Suggestions for Further Reading

ROSKILL COMMISSION, *Commission on the Third London Airport* (London: H.M.S.O., 1970). See also the reading suggested at the end of Chapters 6, 7, 8 and 9, especially those at the end of Chapter 8.

Chapter 13

Resource Costs of Mining Labour

The National Board for Prices and Incomes (P.I.B.) published a study of the resource costs of mining labour as an annex to one of its Coal Price reports [1970]. This illustrated how a divergence between private and social costs might arise in the labour market, and outlined some approaches to this situation. First, let us briefly follow the P.I.B.'s approach and then examine some of the assumptions involved in its analysis.

The P.I.B. maintained that the private and social costs of mining labour differed because some miners are not re-employed as soon as they lose their jobs in the industry, but remain non-productive for a time. In considering the true alternative cost of employing mining labour, it is the contribution to output which the miner would be making if not employed by the National Coal Board which is relevant, and if there is likely to be a time lag before re-employment the discounted value of the alternative output is less than if he can be employed immediately. The P.I.B. assumed in its analysis that the best measure of alternative marginal productivity is the highest payment that a miner is offered outside the coal industry, and that this will correspond to his earnings in mining. Thus it is merely the delay in finding alternative jobs which gives rise to the discrepancy. The

P.I.B. suggested a simplified example to illustrate this principle which showed what alternative production might be sacrificed by delaying redundancies for a year. If one hundred miners are retained in Coal Board employment they clearly cannot be productive in other industries, but if some would otherwise have been unemployed for a period the opportunity cost of their labour in mining is zero during that time. If it is known how long miners are likely to remain unemployed, their probable output (assumed to be proportional to wages) in each time period in other industries can be estimated and discounted back to present value (the P.I.B. used a 10 per cent discount rate). For their hypothetical example the Board supposed that half the miners would find a job within one year, 30 per cent more in the second year and the rest in the third year, and it showed in tabular form (reproduced in Table 6) how output outside mining would be affected by postponing one hundred redundancies for one year. This discounted value can be compared with the present-value output from retaining these one hundred men in mining for a year, which would be a hundred discounted for one year (since all values are assumed to be incurred at year end), that is 90·9. The ratio of these two values $(85·3/90·9 = 93·8\%)$ shows the ratio of resource costs to private costs in this case.

TABLE 6
Number of men re-employed

	Redundancies declared in year 1	Redundancies declared in year 2	Man-years of labour forgone outside coal mining by postponing redundancies	Present value discounted at 10% p.a.
End of year 1	50	—	50	45·5
End of year 2	80	50	30	24·8
End of year 3	100	80	20	15·0
End of year 4	100	100	—	—
				85·3

This example shows how a delay in re-employment can distort the ratio between resource and accounting costs; however, it incorporates a number of assumptions which complicate any attempt at more refined calculations. The boldest is that the marginal productivity of workers in other industries is adequately reflected by their rate of pay; it is extremely difficult to determine how realistic this assumption is because of the problems in measuring marginal productivity. A perfectly competitive labour market would allocate labour to its most productive use, and each employer would pay for labour up to the point at which its marginal productivity equals its cost. However, the existence of substantial imperfections in the labour market, particularly large unions and Government legislation, mean that the wage rate at least is set mainly by non-market institutional considerations. This does not prevent firms from employing labour until its (given) marginal cost equals its marginal productivity, but other constraints are likely to operate here, both in traditional manpower operations and in union resistance to change, which may mean that in practice the marginal equality suggested by the theory fails to hold. Thus the alternative wages of miners may not be an adequate guide to their marginal productivity in other industries. Note that here we have come across a Paretian imperfection in coal wages, and attempts to correct it lead us to suspect more violations of the first-best marginal conditions in other parts of the economy. This is yet further aggravated by taxation, which will typically remove 40 per cent from the marginal wages of workers before they receive them as net earnings; and employers, too, are involved in some employee overheads (National Insurance contributions for example) other than direct wages and salaries. These considerations show the intricate problems of implementing and interpreting Paretian conditions (first and second best) which were so blithely discussed in the early theoretical chapters.

The P.I.B. itself discussed a number of practical problems which might arise, even though it considered rewards to ex-miners, payment by employers and marginal productivity of labour to be adequately correlated for the estimation it suggested. One difficulty was simply ascertaining the appropriate alternative wages for ex-miners, since few data were available on previous experience of redundant coal workers. Using average earnings of workers might be inaccurate because ex-miners are likely to be on average older and less skilled in alternative occupations than a typical local employee. Problems also arise in estimating just how long unemployment is likely to last. For even if a reasonably accurate profile of miners' job prospects can be built up in an area of heavy unemployment like those of many of the pit closures, a redeployed former miner may merely prevent another unemployed worker from taking a job. Thus it is the total effect on unemployment in the area which is relevant, not just the job prospects for the miners themselves. The implications therefore need to be estimated from careful studies of national and regional unemployment, and to take into account Government attempts to relieve such pressures and relocate industry in areas of high and persistent unemployment. Clearly the calculations involved are likely to be complicated and sensitive to changes in these variables.

The P.I.B. report was undertaken at a time when the price of coal was too high to make it competitive at current output, so a decrease in both output and costs was anticipated to optimise the pricing policy and allocation of resources; hence the problems of redundant miners. The change of the coal-industry situation with the increased price of oil in the last few years is a good example of one danger in concentrating too heavily on current problems in devising long-term strategy. For there is a tendency to construct a model allowing for these special difficulties, and to generalise it so that it becomes a basis for calculations even when the problems on which it was based have changed. In other words there may be a discontinuity in the costs and benefits involved in various courses of action which it is easy to ignore. Thus, although in certain situations it is important to allow for the problems that redundant miners experience in finding new employment, it is not appropriate to include social costs lower than accounting costs if the coal industry is expanding and attracting miners away from other industries. In this case the forgone alternative production (on the basis of the assumptions made by the P.I.B.) will be the highest wage they would have been paid outside the coal industry. In constructing a suitable model of real wage costs, therefore, it is necessary to include a discontinuity at the point where the industry expands to attract workers from other jobs. There will of course be an interim stage as the influence of Coal Board demand for labour gradually absorbs the pool of local unemployed. Then, at the stage when further mining labour can be recruited only at the expense of production in other industries, private costs will adequately represent social costs if it is assumed that labour is paid its marginal productivity. (This will be reflected in Table 6 above by a unity ratio between forgone production and mining wages.)

This discontinuity in the case of the coal industry illustrates a general principle of adjusting for market imperfections which arises in another context, the balance of payments. If the market is efficient internationally as well as internally, it can be assumed that the cost of imports is simply the amount of foreign currency needed to buy them. However, at times of large and continuous balance-of-payments deficit, the view is often expressed that imports should be discouraged and exports encouraged, implying that the costs and benefits of these flows are not adequately reflected in their prices. This presumably arises because, if the imbalance does not adjust quickly, the implications (either Government policy to institute internal solutions or the results of international pressure) would incur some social and economic cost not reflected in the accounts. Thus in these circumstances the real benefit of improvements in the balance of payments is greater than the prices alone would indicate. However, such an adjustment would not remain appropriate in the case of a substantial surplus on the balance of payments; in these circumstances, if exports continue to be 'encouraged' at the expense of imports, the imbalance is likely to become even greater. This does have disadvantages, as West Germany and the United States have found since the war, since internal and external liquidity are linked, and large surpluses on the balance of payments may lead to an expansion of money supply at home and so to increased inflation; and it is not likely to be politically popular with our trading partners since we can only run a surplus if at least one other country is in deficit. Thus to encourage exports and discourage imports may be appropriate at times of deficit, but is less so as we approach a balanced situation, and becomes an unsuitable policy if the balance of payments shows significant and persistent surpluses. Such circumstances are often forecast as a result of exploiting the North Sea oil reserves, and it is important to remember that as circumstances change so may the relation between private and social costs and benefits.

To return to the mining example, we have seen how the P.I.B. estimated that the social costs of labour were less than accounting costs in the circumstances then prevailing. This would affect both pricing and investment decisions since using social rather than accounting-cost figures will reduce marginal costs so that the optimum output, at which price equals marginal cost (following the P.I.B.'s assumptions that resources are allocated satisfactorily elsewhere in the economy), will in general be greater. However, so long as wages exceeding alternative marginal product are paid to miners these (higher) accounting costs will not be covered by the price received for coal at the margin; this implies that the industry will incur a greater loss (or smaller profit depending on the relation between average and marginal cost) than would otherwise be the case. Clearly if resource-cost pricing policy is pursued, such implications in terms of subsidy or reduced profit must be accepted by the Government, both as a necessary consequence of the optimum allocation of resources and also as appropriate so far as the distribution of welfare is concerned.

The P.I.B. itself acknowledged that the procedure it had suggested was fraught with practical problems in implementation. Nevertheless it was an interesting illustration in principle of how policy might be affected by using social instead of private costs. The assumptions made about conditions elsewhere in the economy were brave indeed, but we have already seen in Part One that some assumptions need to be made, at least as a basis for estimates, even if the analysis later suggests it is more appropriate to change them. It is by studies of this kind, and the examples we have seen in the last three chapters, that the frontiers of economic knowledge can be extended; however interesting the study of welfare economic theory may be for its own sake, it is only in its application to practical problems such as these that it can be fully interpreted and understood.

Suggestions for Further Reading

NATIONAL BOARD FOR PRICES AND INCOMES, *Coal Prices* (*Second Report*), no. 153, Cmnd. 4455 (London: H.M.S.O., 1970). See also the reading suggested at the end of Chapters 6, 7, 8 and 9.

Bibliography

K. J. ARROW [1966], 'Discounting and Public Investment Criteria', in *Water Resources Research*, ed. A. V. Kneese and S. C. Smith (Baltimore, Johns Hopkins Press).

W. J. BAUMOL [1970], 'On the Discount Rate for Public Projects', in *Public Expenditures and Policy Analysis*, ed. R. H. Haveman and J. Margolis (Chicago, Markham).

W. J. BAUMOL [1972], *Economic Theory and Operations Analysis*, 3rd edn (Englewood Cliffs, N.J., Prentice-Hall).

M. E. BEESLEY [1965], 'The Value of Time Spent in Travelling: Some New Evidence', *Economica*, vol. 32.

M. E. BEESLEY and M. Q. DALVI [1973], 'The Journey to Work and Cost Benefit Analysis', in *Cost Benefit and Cost Effectiveness*, ed. J. N. Wolfe (London, Allen & Unwin).

M. E. BEESLEY and C. D. FOSTER [1965], 'The Victoria Line: Social Benefits and Finances', *Journal of the Royal Statistical Society*, series B, vol. 128.

ABRAM BERGSON [1966], *Essays in Normative Economics* (The Belknap Press of Harvard University Press).

K. E. BOULDING [1948], 'Welfare Economics', in *A Survey of Contemporary Economics*, vol. 2, ed. The American Economic Association (Blakiston).

D. BRAYBROOKE [1954–5], 'Farewell to the New Welfare Economics', *Review of Economic Studies*, vol. 22.

S. B. CHASE JR (ED.) [1968], *Problems in Public Expenditure*, Brookings Institution (London, Allen & Unwin).

E. W. CLEMENS [1941], 'Price Discrimination in Decreasing Cost Industries', *American Economic Review*, vol. 31.

R. H. COASE [1946], 'The Marginal Cost Controversy', *Economica*, vol. 13.

DAVID COOMBES [1971], *State Enterprise*, Political and Economic Planning (London, Allen & Unwin).

G. CORTI [1973], 'Risk, Uncertainty and Cost Benefit: Some Notes on

Practical Difficulties for Project Appraisals', in *Cost Benefit and Cost Effectiveness*, ed. J. N. Wolfe (London, Allen & Unwin).

K. W. DAM [1964], 'Oil and Gas Licensing in the North Sea', *Journal of Law and Economics*, vol. 7.

K. W. DAM [1970], 'The Pricing of North Sea Gas in Britain', *Journal of Law and Economics*, vol. 13.

OTTO ECKSTEIN [1958], *Water Resources Development* (Harvard University Press).

I. EVERINGHAM, D. GUILLEBAUD, T. JONES AND J. STORY [1975], *North Sea Oil: Its Effect on Britain's Economic Future* (Fontainebleau, European Institute of Business Administration, June).

M. S. FELDSTEIN [1964], 'Net Social Benefits and the Public Investment Decision', *Oxford Economic Papers*, vol. 16.

M. S. FELDSTEIN AND J. M. FLEMING [1964], 'The Problem of Time-Stream Evaluation: Present Value versus Internal Rate of Return Rules', *Bulletin of the Oxford University Institute of Economics and Statistics*, vol. 26.

J. M. FLEMING [1944], 'Price and Output Policy of State Enterprise', *Economic Journal*, vol. 54.

J. K. GALBRAITH [1974], *The New Industrial State*, 2nd edn (Harmondsworth, Penguin).

H.M. GOVERNMENT [1948], *Gas Act* (London, H.M.S.O.).

H.M. GOVERNMENT [1961], *The Financial and Economic Obligations of the Nationalised Industries*, Cmnd. 1337 (London, H.M.S.O.).

H.M. GOVERNMENT [1965], *Prices and Incomes Policy*, Cmnd. 2639 (London, H.M.S.O.).

H.M. GOVERNMENT [1965], *The National Plan*, Cmnd. 2764 (London, H.M.S.O.).

H.M. GOVERNMENT [1965], *Fuel Policy*, Cmnd. 2798 (London, H.M.S.O.).

H.M. GOVERNMENT [1967], *Nationalised Industries: A Review of Economic and Financial Objectives*, Cmnd. 3437 (London, H.M.S.O.).

H.M. GOVERNMENT [1969], *Ministerial Control of the Nationalised Industries*, Cmnd. 4027 (London, H.M.S.O.).

H. A. J. GREEN [1961], 'The Social Optimum in the Presence of Monopoly and Taxation', *Review of Economic Studies*, vol. 29.

J. R. HICKS [1939], 'Foundations of Welfare Economics', *Economic Journal*, vol. 49.

HAROLD HOTELLING [1938], 'The General Welfare in Relation to Problems of Taxation and of Railway and Utility Rates', *Econometrica*, vol. 6.

H. S. HOUTHAKKER [1951], 'Electricity Tariffs in Theory and Practice', *Economic Journal*, vol. 61.

N. KALDOR [1939], 'Welfare Propositions', *Economic Journal,* vol. 49.

F. H. KNIGHT [1921], *Risk, Uncertainty and Profit* (New York, Harper & Row).

W. A. LEWIS [1941], 'The Two-part Tariff and The Two-part Tariff: a Reply', *Economica,* vol. 8.

R. G. LIPSEY and R. K. LANCASTER [1957], 'The General Theory of the Second Best', *Review of Economic Studies,* vol. 24.

I. M. D. LITTLE [1957], *A Critique of Welfare Economics* (Oxford University Press).

M. McMANUS, 'Comments on the General Theory of the Second Best', *Review of Economic Studies,* vol. 26 (1959).

S. A. MARGLIN [1963], 'The Social Rate of Discount and the Optimum Rate of Investment', *Quarterly Journal of Economics,* vol. 77.

A. J. MERRET AND A. SYKES [1963], *The Finance and Analysis of Capital Projects* (London, Longmans).

E. J. MISHAN [1972], *Elements of Cost Benefit Analysis* (London, Allen & Unwin).

NATIONAL BOARD FOR PRICES AND INCOMES [1968], *Third General Report,* no. 77, Cmnd. 3715 (London, H.M.S.O.).

NATIONAL BOARD FOR PRICES AND INCOMES [1969], *Gas Prices,* no. 102, Cmnd. 3924 (London, H.M.S.O.).

NATIONAL BOARD FOR PRICES AND INCOMES [1970], *Coal Prices (Second Report),* no. 153, Cmnd. 4455 (London, H.M.S.O.).

J. R. NELSON (ED.) [1964], *Marginal Cost Pricing in Practice* (Englewood Cliffs, N.J., Prentice-Hall).

VILFREDO PARETO [1972], *Manual of Political Economy,* trans. Ann S. Schwier and Alfred N. Page (London, Macmillan); originally published in Italian *circa* 1909.

D. W. PEARCE [1971], *Cost Benefit Analysis* (London, Macmillan).

M. V. POSNER [1973], *Fuel Policy: A Study in Applied Economics* (London, Macmillan).

A. R. PREST AND R. TURVEY [1966], 'Cost Benefit Analysis: A Survey', in *Surveys of Economic Theory,* vol. 3 (London, Macmillan).

C. M. PRICE [1973], 'Marginal Cost Pricing and Its Application to Domestic Gas Tariffs', doctoral thesis presented to Nottingham University.

RICHARD PRYKE [1971], *Public Enterprise in Practice: The British Experience of Nationalisation over Two Decades* (London, MacGibbon & Kee).

J. R. QUIRK AND R. SAPOSNIK [1968], *General Equilibrium Theory and Welfare Economics* (New York, McGraw-Hill).

G. L. REID AND K. ALLEN [1970], *Nationalised Industries* (Harmondsworth, Penguin).

G. L. REID, K. ALLEN AND D. J. HARRIS [1973], *The Nationalised Fuel*

Industries (London, Heinemann).

ROSKILL COMMISSION [1970], *Commission on the Third London Airport* (London, H.M.S.O.).

NANCY RUGGLES [1949–50], 'Recent Developments in the Theory of Marginal Cost Pricing', *Review of Economic Studies*, vol. 17.

T. SCITOVSKY [1941–2], 'A Note on Welfare Propositions in Economics', *Review of Economic Studies*, vol. 9.

SELECT COMMITTEE ON NATIONALISED INDUSTRIES [1975], *Nationalised Industries and the Exploitation of North Sea Oil and Gas*, H.C.P. 345 (London, H.M.S.O., April).

RALPH TURVEY [1963], 'Present Value vs. Internal Rate of Return', *Economic Journal*, vol. 57.

RALPH TURVEY (ED.) [1968], *Public Enterprise* (Harmondsworth, Penguin).

RALPH TURVEY [1968], *Optimal Pricing and Investment in Electricity Supply* (London, Allen & Unwin).

RALPH TURVEY [1971], *Economic Analysis and Public Enterprises* (London, Allen & Unwin).

P. WATSON AND N. MANSFIELD [1973], 'The Valuation of Time in Cost–Benefit Studies', in *Cost Benefit and Cost Effectiveness*, ed. J. N. Wolfe (London, Allen & Unwin).

ALAN WILLIAMS [1973], 'Cost Benefit Analysis: Bastard Science And/or Insidious Poison in the Body Politick?', in *Cost Benefit and Cost Effectiveness*, ed. J. N. Wolfe (London, Allen & Unwin).

O. E. WILLIAMSON [1966], 'Peak-load Pricing and Optimal Capacity Under Indivisibility Constraints', *American Economic Review*, vol. 56.

D. M. WINCH [1965], 'Consumer's Surplus and the Compensation Principle', *American Economic Review*, vol. 55.

D. M. WINCH [1971], *Analytical Welfare Economics* (Harmondsworth, Penguin).

J. N. WOLFE (ED.) [1973], *Cost Benefit and Cost Effectiveness* (London, Allen & Unwin).

Index